ATLANTAboy: An Insider's Guide to Gay Atlanta. Copyright © 2005 by Mega Niche Media. Manufactured in the United States of America. All rights reserved. No part of this book may be reproduced or transmitted in any form or by any means, electronic or mechanical, including photocopying, recording, or by an information storage and retrieval system—except by a reviewer who may quote brief passages in a review. Published by Mega Niche Media, 925-B Peachtree Street #398, Atlanta, GA 30309. 404-745-8636. First edition.

Visit ATLANTAboy.com for additional news, information, and updated information on gay Atlanta.

Although the author and publisher have made every effort to ensure the accuracy and completeness of the information contained in this book, we assume no responsibility for errors, inaccuracies, omissions, or any inconsistency herein. Any slight of people, places, or organizations is unintentional.

ISBN 0-9707095-6-0
Library of Congress Control Number 2005924264

Edited by Nick Street, nickstreetis@yahoo.com
Cover by Paul Wolski, AlterEgoPopArt.com

ATTENTION: Quantity discounts are available on bulk purchases of this book for reselling, educational purposes, subscription incentives, gifts, or fund raising. Special books or book excerpts can also be created to fit specific needs. For information, please contact our Special Sales Department at Mega Niche Media, 925-B Peachtree Street #398, Atlanta, GA 30309. 404-745-8636.

dedication

This book is dedicated to everyone in Atlanta—gay, straight, and everything in between—who makes it such a wonderful place to live, work and play!

— Alex!

Happy Birthday, I hope you have a good and gay year. When I asked Kate what you like to read she said anything gay so... you're welcome! Anyway you're a delight to be around and anyone who makes Kate as happy as you do, is a dear friend of mine..

As Ever,
Eli

acknowledgments

The authors would like to thank the following people for their generous support and faithful encouragement:

Nick Street at Alyson Books, Paul Wolski at Alter Ego Pop Art, Mr. Charlie Brown at Charlie Brown's Cabaret, "Bubba D. Licious"/Jim Marks at The Names Project Foundation, Philip Rafshoon at Outwrite Bookstore & Coffeehouse, Gregory Pierce at the Atlanta Convention and Visitors Bureau, Tray Butler at *David Atlanta*, Christopher Kind at The Masquerade, Michael Alvear of *Men Are Pigs, But We Love Bacon*, Elise Tedeschi at The Reynolds Group, Brad Williams at Jungle and Red Chair Video Lounge, Mike Fleming at *Southern Voice*, Damien Childes at Red Chair Restaurant and Video Lounge, Len Evans at Project Publicity, Cindy L. Abel at BizVox Marketing Communications, the entire staff at BookMasters, everyone at Mega Niche Media, and all of our friends and family.

contents

	Welcome to Atlanta	**3**
	Metro Atlanta Map	4
	Midtown Atlanta Map	6
	Foreword by Bubba D. Licious	8
	Introduction by Mr. Charlie Brown	10
	Neighborhoods	**13**
	Ansley Park / Midtown	13
	Piedmont Park	14
	Annual Events at Piedmont Park	16
	Cabbagetown	18
	Candler Park	19
	Decatur	20
	Downtown	20
	Underground Atlanta	21
	Druid Hills	22
	Grant Park	22
	Inman Park	23
	Little Five Points	24
	Virginia-Highlands	25
	Celebrities	**26**
	Reside in Atlanta	26
	Born or Raised in Atlanta	26
	Studied in Atlanta	27

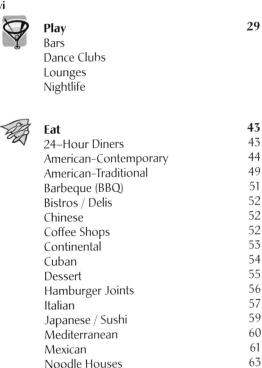

Play	**29**
Bars	
Dance Clubs	
Lounges	
Nightlife	
Eat	**43**
24–Hour Diners	43
American-Contemporary	44
American-Traditional	49
Barbeque (BBQ)	51
Bistros / Delis	52
Chinese	52
Coffee Shops	52
Continental	53
Cuban	54
Dessert	55
Hamburger Joints	56
Italian	57
Japanese / Sushi	59
Mediterranean	60
Mexican	61
Noodle Houses	63
Pizza	64
Seafood	64
Southern	65
Southwestern	67
Spanish / Tapas	69
Specialty Grocery Stores	70
Steakhouses	72
Thai	72
Vietnamese	73

vii

Shop 75
Antique Stores
Boutiques
Malls
Shops
Storefronts

Watch 87
Art Museums
Ballet
Cabarets
Cinemas
Concerts
Operas
Playhouses
Symphonies
Theatres

Visit 97
Attractions
Gardens
Historic Sites
Museums
Tours
Zoos

Sweat 105
Fitness Centers
Gyms
Health Clubs
Yoga Studios

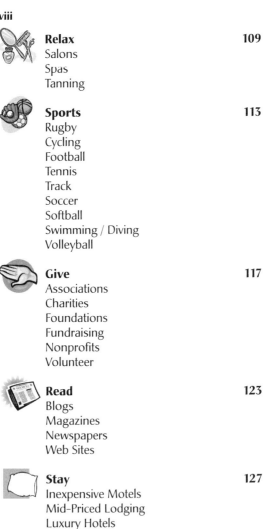

Relax — 109
Salons
Spas
Tanning

Sports — 113
Rugby
Cycling
Football
Tennis
Track
Soccer
Softball
Swimming / Diving
Volleyball

Give — 117
Associations
Charities
Foundations
Fundraising
Nonprofits
Volunteer

Read — 123
Blogs
Magazines
Newspapers
Web Sites

Stay — 127
Inexpensive Motels
Mid-Priced Lodging
Luxury Hotels

Bed & Breakfasts
Youth Hostels

Annual Events 131
January
February
March
April
May
June
July
August
September
October
November
December

Worship 137
Baptist
Catholic
Christian
Episcopal
Jewish
Lutheran
Methodist
Metropolitan Community Church (MCC)
Presbyterian
Unitarian Universalist
Unity

Resources 141
Airlines
Alcohol & Drug Dependency
Animals

Automobiles
City of Atlanta
Consumer Complaints & Services
County Office
Crime
Discrimination
Garbage & Sanitation
Government & Elected Officials
Entertainment
Health & Medical Care
Physician Referral Service
Legal Referral
Libraries
Parks
Parking Violations
Police
Post Office
Recycling
Shipping Services
Sports
State Government
Taxi Service
Time
Tourism & Travel
Traffic / Road Conditions
Transportation
Utility Emergencies
Venues
Weather
Zip Codes

About the Authors   152

Index   154

In This Chapter

Welcome to Atlanta • Metro Atlanta Map • Midtown Atlanta Map • Foreword by Bubba D. Licious • Introduction by Mr. Charlie Brown

welcome to atlanta

Whether you're planning a trip to Atlanta, just visiting, or thinking about moving here, there are many reasons to come to the South's gay capital (besides the boys!). Our city may have burned to the ground during the Civil War, but today it's growing faster than ever. Almost five million people—many of them gay—live in the Atlanta area. In fact, most of the attractions you'll want to visit are located in and around Midtown, which also happens to be the city's gay epicenter (how convenient!).

There you'll find the home of *Gone with the Wind* author Margaret Mitchell, the fabulous Fox Theatre, Piedmont Park, and the Atlanta Botanical Gardens. And right next door Downtown you'll find Charlie Brown's Cabaret (home to Atlanta's hottest drag queens), CNN Center, The World of Coca-Cola (both of which offer a great tour) and Centennial Olympic Park (see listings under *Visit*). Along with one of the largest gay scenes in the country, Atlanta also has a rich gay history. Until now, there was no travel guide devoted exclusively to gay Atlanta—that's why we decided to create *ATLANTAboy*.

Although *ATLANTAboy* is by no means a complete guide to the entire city, we've made sure to include most of the gay and gay-friendly hotspots that abound here. Stick to the places we mention inside and you're sure to have an amazing time. Even if you're already located in Atlanta, you're bound to find somewhere new and exciting to explore. We sure did, even after living here for over 20 years! We even decided to mention lots of "Insider Tips" that you won't find anywhere else. These are things we've discovered—sometimes the hard way—that we wanted to pass on to help make your visit here a little easier and perhaps a whole lot more fun! Have a blast, be safe, and enjoy the city we call home.

Welcome,

Jordan McAuley & Matt Burkhalter

metro atlanta

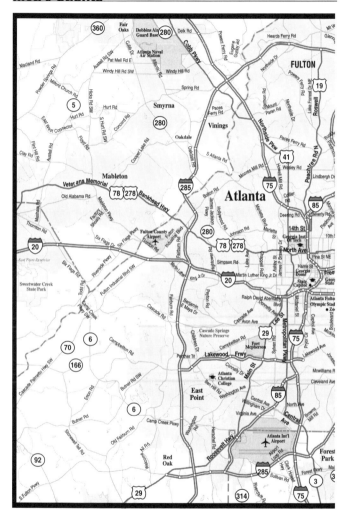

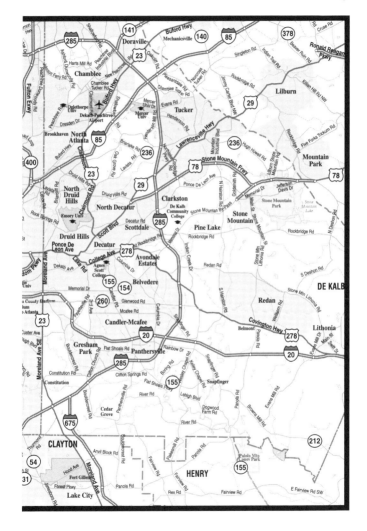

midtown atlanta

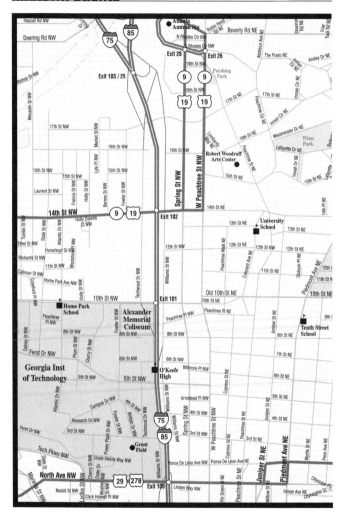

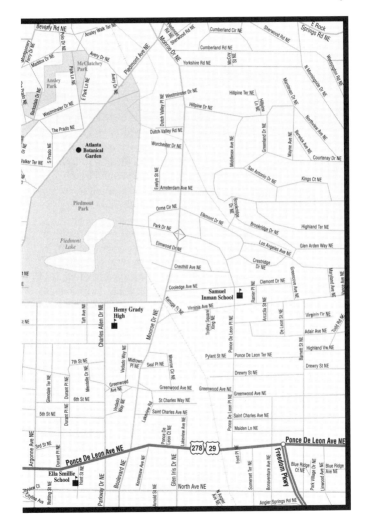

foreword

I had grown up in Savannah, Georgia and had spent almost ten years on Hilton Head Island after graduating from college. In early 1989, after almost ten years of internal struggles and identity issues, I decided I had to make a move in order to find myself. Since I wanted to move to a bigger city, I chose Atlanta because I wanted to remain in the South and because I loved the Atlanta Braves.

Sixteen years later, I know now that there was—and is—no better place on earth for me than this peachy metropolis. Atlanta offered me the opportunity to have a successful career in accounting and finance, but my social life and philanthropic opportunities are what really caused me to fall in love with the city.

My first summer in Atlanta, I was a member of the Armory softball team. When they dared me to perform drag for the first time, I took them up on the challenge. That's when "Bubba D. Licious" was born. "Bubba" quickly became a campy, comedic hit among the cast of the world-famous Armorettes (see listing under *Give*) who were better known as "The Camp Drag Queens of the South".

Every Sunday at the Armory (see listing under *Play*), we performed comedy shows to packed rooms of the wonderful gay men and women of our city. During this time we received a wonderful amount of generosity and support from the Atlanta community as we raised millions of

foreword

dollars for HIV, AIDS, and other community causes. This tradition proudly continues.

The gay community in Atlanta has grown to become one of the largest in this country. Almost every young person who comes out in the South moves to Atlanta or visits frequently. The diversity of our community reaches all, and I am thrilled to have been a resident and fundraiser in such a great city.

ATLANTAboy will give you a lot of insider information on gay Atlanta and the people that help make it great. Enjoy the book and visit our city often. Whatever your pleasure, there's nothing like a little South in your mouth!

Love & lashes,

Bubba D. Licious

Bubba D. Licious
BubbaDLicious.net

introduction

No other city in the South is as economically powerful, as ethnically diverse, and as historically rich as Atlanta.

First known as Terminus, a rail-hub before the War Between the States, Atlanta is now the heart of the New South's gay culture. Atlanta's gay and lesbian community, the largest in the Southeast, offers a degree of freedom and a wealth of experience that can't be found anywhere else. Tens of thousands of gays from across America and around the world visit our city each year. Most of them happily return, many of them never leave.

Gay businesses also abound in Atlanta. From our vibrant nightlife—which I'm particularly proud of—to our shops, galleries, restaurants, and lodging, visitors have a veritable smorgasbord of delights from which to choose. At my self-named drag venue, Charlie Brown's Cabaret (see listing under *Play*), I've been host to thousands of first-time visitors to our city over the years. It's been my pleasure to be an unofficial "Atlanta Ambassador" for our community.

introduction

So, welcome to Atlanta! Experience our city's vibrant gay culture. Enjoy our gentle Southern hospitality. You'll be glad you did.

Charlie Brown

Mr. Charlie Brown
CharlieBrownsCabaret.net

In This Chapter

Ansley Park / Midtown • Cabbagetown • Candler Park •
Decatur • Downtown • Druid Hills • Grant Park • Inman
Park • Little Five Points • Underground Atlanta •
Piedmont Park • Virginia-Highlands

neighborhoods

ANSLEY PARK / MIDTOWN

AnsleyPark.org / MidtownAtlanta.org

Developed in 1904, Ansley Park was Atlanta's first commuter suburb. The home of Piedmont Park (see below), the neighborhood of Ansley Park / Midtown is also the center of Atlanta's thriving gay community, as most of the bars, restaurants, and stores in the area are gay-owned or gay-friendly. In the 1960s and 70s, many hippies migrated to Midtown to take advantage of its low-cost housing, making it the largest "hippie district" in the Southeast! Times change, and many high-end stores, luxury apartments, and upscale condominiums flourished in the area shortly after the 1996 Summer Olympics.

Midtown is home to many people who like to march to the beat of their own drummer. One of these colorful characters is "Baton Bob," a self-described "costumed entertainer." You'll know he's near when you hear his whistle or see him performing in one of his colorful costumes. "Baton Bob's" mission is to bring a little joy to your day, so make sure you smile, honk, and wave!

ATLANTA QUICK FACTS

Metropolitan Area: 131 square miles

Population: 5 million

Elevation: 1,035 feet

Average Annual Rainfall: 48 inches

Average January Temperature: 48 degrees F

Average July Temperature: 90 degrees F

Major Industries: high tech, transportation, financial services

Ethnic Mix: 61% African American, 33% Caucasian, 4% Hispanic, 2% Asian

Time Zone: GMT -5

Area Codes: 404, 770, 678 (must be included when dialing locally)

PIEDMONT PARK

PiedmontPark.org

In 1887, Benjamin Walker sold 189 acres of land to the Gentleman's Driving Club (which is now known as the Piedmont Driving Club). Although the property was supposed to be used to create an exclusive club and horse racing grounds, the new owners leased the land to the

neighborhoods

Piedmont Exposition Company, which created a fairgrounds and exposition area named Piedmont Park. The best-known exposition held at the park was the Cotton States International Exposition of 1895, which was essentially a World's Fair. This event helped turn the park into what it is today. The ball fields were originally a horse racetrack, and a nearby spring was excavated to create Lake Clara Meer, where residents once swam and sunbathed.

When the city of Atlanta purchased the park in 1904, it was considered too far from the city to be useful to most of its citizens. But with the expansion and growth of the city, Piedmont Park has become a welcome green space for city residents. In 1909, the sons of Frederick Law Olmsted (who designed Central Park in New York City) were hired to create a master plan for the park. But the plan was never fully implemented due to funding issues. Recent renovations and expansions taken from the Olmsted's plan have made the park a more beautiful resource for the community.

Today, Piedmont Park is a much-needed oasis in Midtown where ATLANTAboys (as well as their straight friends and family) can relax and play. Although it is relatively quiet in the winter, during the summer months you'll see folks doing everything from playing volleyball, football, soccer, and other sports to simply enjoying a game of catch with their dogs or attending a festival (see listing). At over 180 acres, Piedmont Park is Atlanta's largest park and has played host to many celebrities—from John Philip Sousa in 1895 to Oprah Winfrey in 2004.

DID YOU KNOW?

Did you know that motion picture projection made its U.S. debut at Piedmont Park's Cotton States and International Exhibition in 1895? In a small booth called "Living Pictures," patrons could see moving images projected onto a screen. The process was called Phantoscope, which was different from Thomas Edison's Kinetoscope box (where only one person could watch at a time). After the exposition was over, Edison bought the rights to Phantoscope, renamed the process Vitascope, and took credit for the invention.

Source: *Piedmont Park: Celebrating Atlanta's Common Ground*

MARTA

If you need a ride, MARTA (Metropolitan Atlanta Rapid Transit Authority) offers bus and rail service throughout the city. It serves over 109 million passengers on over 47 miles of rail each year. *ItsMARTA.com*

Annual Events at Piedmont Park

Atlanta Pride
June 24 - 26

The first Atlanta Gay Pride celebration was actually a rally held on June 27, 1970 when about 100 members of the

Gay Liberation Front and the Gay Activist Alliance attended. Over the past 24 years, the celebration has expanded to include over 320,000 attendees. The park becomes the central gathering spot during Pride weekend, but there are many concerts, rallies, and parties scattered all over the city from Friday to Sunday. On Sunday—the last day of Pride—the parade traditionally starts in the morning, and the party goes strong until the closing Starlight Cabaret ceremony at the park. *404-929-0071, AtlantaPride.org*

Atlanta Symphony Orchestra
June & August (Various Dates)

The Atlanta Symphony Orchestra performs two concerts—one in June and another in August—especially for dog lovers (and their dogs of course!) called "Bark in the Park." Be prepared for an evening of barefoot-in-the-park elegance and culture . . . how Southern! *404-733-4900, AtlantaSymphony.com*

Insider Tip: Bring some sparklers for the traditional finale!

Dogwood Festival
April 8–10

The Atlanta Dogwood Festival is quite the tradition at Piedmont Park. The annual springtime event is a celebration of arts and entertainment. The park is filled with booths from artists from around the United States. *404-817-6642, Dogwood.org*

Insider Tip: Be sure to pick up your free dogwood seedling plant to take home!

Screen on the Green
Thursdays in June

Turner Classic Movies sponsors this weekly screening of classic films during the month of June. Showtime starts at sundown on Thursday evenings and traditionally begins with a Looney Toon cartoon. Often celebrities are on hand to introduce their respective films. In 2004 Atlanta resident Jane Fonda and her guest Robert Redford introduced "Barefoot in the Park" and Cloris Leachman introduced "Young Frankenstein." It's great fun to scream "No more wire hangers!" with Joan Crawford . . . and a couple thousand other movie goers. *404-878-2600, Turner.com/ScreenOnTheGreen*

Insider Tip: Bring a picnic dinner, a bottle of wine, lots of friends—and something to sit on if it recently rained!

CABBAGETOWN

Cabbagetown.org

Founded in 1885 as a community for the Fulton Bag & Cotton Mill's workers, Cabbagetown was one of Atlanta's original industrial settlements. Although some of the area's residents swear that the neighborhood's real name is "Mill Town," the story behind Cabbagetown is a local myth to this day. Once upon a time, a Model T truck tipped over at the intersection of Boulevard onto Carroll, spilling its cargo of cabbage into the streets. Since it was a poor mill town, the residents claimed the cabbage as payment for helping put the Ford back on all four wheels. Since cabbage cannot be overcooked—it just gets softer over time—the workers left it boiling all day, imparting a "distinct" smell to the area. Thus the name Cabbagetown was born.

Although the mill hasn't operated since the 1970s, today Cabbagetown is an area of tremendous growth. The mill itself has been renovated into the nation's largest residential loft community—the Fulton Cotton Mill Lofts—which houses everyone from artists and musicians to business professionals. You'll also find popular restaurants like Agave and Six Feet Under (see listings) as well as the historic Oakland Cemetery, where many of Atlanta's most famous residents including Margaret Mitchell are buried.

CANDLER PARK

CandlerPark.org

Originally a Union camp during the Civil War, the area known as Edgewood (which later became Candler Park) was formed in 1890. Soon after the war, Edgewood began to prosper with its own government, schools, and utilities until 1908, when its citizens decided they wanted to be part of the city of Atlanta. In the 1920s, Asa Candler had the area graded to fill in a large valley and remove a hill, which destroyed many of the original homes in the area but created Candler Park.

In the 1960s, the neighborhood began to flourish again and never slowed down. In the 1970s and 80s, Candler Park became popular with lesbians, who purchased many of the neighborhood's craftsman bungalow homes before real estate prices went up. Today, Candler Park "nurtures the eclectic"—residents include poets, activists, musicians, lawyers, and business professionals. Candler Park's small but thriving business district is also one of the most gay-friendly areas of town, with great eateries like Fellini's Pizza and the Flying Biscuit (see listings).

DECATUR

DecaturGA.com

Founded in 1823, the city of Decatur was named after U.S. naval hero Stephen Decatur. It is the second oldest municipality in the metropolitan Atlanta area. The main downtown courthouse square, which is located where two Indian trails once crossed, is still a gathering place for the community and its many festivals. Although there were plans to make the city a major stop on the new Western and Atlantic Railroad line in the 1830s, local residents objected because they feared the noise and pollution from the rail line would be too much for them to bear. So, the railroad moved to a small city called Terminus, which later became Atlanta.

Today, Decatur is a small city of 18,000 six miles east of downtown Atlanta. Known for its thriving performing arts and music scene (the Indigo Girls got their start here), the city is also home to many fabulous restaurants. Decatur is a very gay-friendly area.

DOWNTOWN

Founded as a rail terminus (and thus named Terminus), Atlanta was originally a small, rugged railroad crossing. A few years later, the city was renamed Marthasville and began to grow. To match its aspirations, the city was given a more dramatic name: Atlanta. After General Sherman burned the city in September 1864, Atlantans returned to rebuild their neighborhoods from the smok-

neighborhoods

ing ruins. Like a Phoenix rising from the ashes (the Phoenix is also the city's symbol), Atlanta came back stronger than ever.

Today Downtown is home to attractions like Underground Atlanta (see below), the World of Coca-Cola, Centennial Olympic Park and CNN Center (see listings). Downtown is also the headquarters of many large corporations such as Coca-Cola, CNN, Delta Air Lines, Equifax, CDC (National Center for Disease Control and Prevention) and TBS (Turner Broadcasting System). It's also the home of Georgia State University.

UNDERGROUND ATLANTA

Underground-Atlanta.com

Located in the heart of downtown and covering six city blocks, Underground Atlanta was once a just a rail yard. Over time, however, the city built up and over the rail lines. When the tracks were no longer needed, the abandoned sublevel was turned into a mixed-use development. Thus Underground Atlanta was born.

Today there are over 100 specialty stores, restaurants, and bars in Underground (as it's known to locals). Recent additions are Future—a high-energy dance club (which is gay on Wednesdays)—and Charlie Brown's Cabaret (which features New Orleans-style drag performances by Atlanta's hottest drag queens). You'll also find the Alley Cat (a rock and roll restaurant and bar), Latin Sol (a salsa club with the largest wooden dance floor in Atlanta), Island Oasis (a show bar), Koco's Latin Restaurant and Bar (a Caribbean restaurant and karaoke bar), Jamaica Jamaica (a restaurant and bar with live reggae), and Irish Bred (an Irish pub.) A special exception to the city laws allows you to go from bar to bar with drink in hand until 4 a.m. (Bars in other parts of the city must close by 3 a.m. and public consumption of alcohol is prohibited). (See listings for Future and Charlie Brown's Cabaret under *Play*.)

DRUID HILLS

DruidHills.org

Druid Hills was designed in 1893 by Frederick Law Olmsted, one of America's most famous landscape architects (who also designed Central Park in New York City). The park-like area is filled with many large, elegant homes by noted architects such as Neel Reid, W.T. Downing, and Philip Shutze. This leafy neighborhood was the inspiration for the Academy Award-winning film *Driving Miss Daisy*. If you keep your eyes open, you may even spy Miss Daisy's home, which is located on Lullwater Avenue. Druid Hills is also located near the Fernbank Museum of Natural History (see listing), a great stop if you love nature and science.

GRANT PARK

GrantPark.org

Grant Park was given to the city of Atlanta in 1883 by entrepreneur Lemuel P. Grant, who is described as one of the founding fathers of Atlanta. In addition to acting as

neighborhoods 23

an agent of both the Western and Atlantic Railroad and the Georgia Seaboard Air Line Railroad (which intersected at Terminus), Grant also served as an engineer during the Civil War. He helped plan the Confederate Army's defensive lines around Atlanta and continued to serve the city as a member of the city council and as one of the authors of a new city charter in 1873.

After several decades of steady development, Grant Park and the surrounding neighborhoods were devastated by the construction of Interstate 20, which split the area in two. Recently revitalized, Grant Park has become one of the first Atlanta neighborhoods to spur a rebirth of the "intown" area. In the year 2000 it was named the largest historic district in Atlanta. The neighborhood's families—both gay and straight—have made Grant Park one of Atlanta's most beloved communities.

INMAN PARK

InmanPark.org

After serving as ground zero for many Civil War battles, Inman Park became Atlanta's first planned community thanks to entrepreneur Joel Hurt. Hurt believed people should live in a park-like setting convenient to a central business district. In keeping with Hurt's vision, homes and mansions in Inman Park were built on large lots with plenty of space. In 1889, Hurt built more than 300 Victorian-style homes in the area that have since been beautifully restored to resemble San Francisco's "painted ladies." Green spaces like Springvale Park, designed by the Olmsted Brothers, were also built. Hurt also designed one of the nation's first "rapid transit systems" (the original trolley barn still stands today).

In the early 1900s, the increasing popularity of the automobile inspired residents to move into Atlanta's newly developed suburbs, which drained much of the vitality from Inman Park. In 1970, however, a rebirth began when "urban pioneers" restored 40 homes in the area. Despite the threat of a new highway and the demolition of many homes, the area has continued to flourish as a reminder of the city's original beauty. Today Inman Park attracts gay residents who are looking for a respite from the hustle-and-bustle of Midtown. It is also convenient to Freedom Parkway, the Jimmy Carter Presidential Library, and Little Five Points (see listings).

LITTLE FIVE POINTS

L5P.com

Little Five Points shares a history with Inman Park. When Joel Hurt's Atlanta Street Railroad Company was formed, Edgewood Avenue became a road for the tracks. Around 1908, the area of Little Five Points (where five train tracks intersected) developed into a commercial area that thrived until the 1950s, when homeowners moved away to escape the new I-20 freeway. A quick downfall ensued, and by the end of the 60s the area had become seedy and neglected. In the 1970s, however, renovations and a clean-up effort began in conjunction with the revitalization of surrounding areas. Led by several businesses that still stand today, Little Five Points began to thrive again while still preserving the eclectic flavor that Li'l Five is known for.

neighborhoods

Located between Inman Park and Candler Park, Little Five Points today is a bohemian retail area that's home to a variety of distinctive stores and restaurants. It's not unusual to find a hippie or two hanging out or granola-types eating organic and vegetarian fare at area restaurants like the Flying Biscuit (see listing). Little Five Points is also home to denizens of the alternative music scene (Outkast got their start here) who shop for vintage clothes, vinyl records, tattoos, and piercings in the area's laid-back shops.

VIRGINIA-HIGHLANDS

VaHi.org

In 1925, the Atlanta Street Railway Company began selling pieces of land for suburban development. Developers bought large plots and divided them into areas for residential and commercial use. This growth continued steadily until the 1960s, when most of the city's original suburbs including the Highlands began to decline.

In the 1970s, the Highlands were swept up in a wave of revitalization that was also bringing new life to surrounding areas. Proposed freeway construction threatened to crush this renaissance, but the idea was defeated by the community. In 1988, John Howell Park on Virginia Avenue was dedicated to the memory of Highlands resident John Howell, one of the many residents who fought hard to stop the development of I-485. The park occupies three acres of land where 11 homes were demolished for the proposed highway. Howell died from complications of HIV in 1988.

ATLANTA CELEBRITIES

Reside in Atlanta:
Dallas Austin
Elton John
Indigo Girls
Jane Fonda
Janet Jackson
Jermaine Dupri
Ludacris
Outkast
Shaquille O'Neal
Shawn Mullins
Ted Turner
TLC
Usher
Whitney Houston & Bobby Brown

Born or Raised in Atlanta:
Amy Ray (Indigo Girls)
Amanda Bearse
Andre 3000 (Outkast)
Dakota Fanning
Dallas Austin
Diana DeGarmo
Eric Lively
Fred Schneider (B-52's)
Gale Harold
Jeff Foxworthy
Jermaine Dupri
John Mayer
Julia Roberts
Kim Basinger
Holly Hunter

Hulk Hogan
Little Richard
Nancy Grace
Pat Conroy
Randy Harrison
Raven Symone
Rozonda "Chilli" Thomas (TLC)
RuPaul
Rusty Joiner
Ryan Seacrest
Shawn Mullins
Stephen Dorff
Usher

Studied in Atlanta:
Spike Lee (Morehouse College)
Kenneth Cole (Emory University)

Source: *ContactAnyCelebrity.com*

Did You Know?

Both lead stars of Showtime's *Queer As Folk*—Gale Harold (Brian Kinney) and Randy Harrison (Justin Taylor)—grew up in Atlanta.

In This Chapter

Bars • Dance Clubs • Lounges • Nightlife

play

Playing is a full-time occupation for many ATLANTAboys—and with so many clubs and bars, why not? There's a place to cater to every kind of interest. Most of us here just throw on a fitted graphic T-shirt and some jeans and run out the door, but the more adventurous boys can strap on a harness or some chaps and still find a place to strut their stuff for the evening.

ARMORY – If you want it, chances are you're going to find it at the Armory. The dance floor allows you to swirl and twirl, but if you're not quite coordinated enough for that, there are pool tables as well as an enclosed patio with a nice view of the Midtown skyline. The Armory was originally the home of the Armorettes camp drag shows (see listing under *Give*) which raised money for the gay community. *836 Juniper Street (6th Street), 404-881-9280*

Insider Tip: The Armory recently made national headlines when the musical revue *Naked Boys Singing* (which is performed at the club) was shut down by police for its nudity. The show was later allowed to reopen after the police admitted they'd made a mistake. Visit NakedBoysSingingAtlanta.com for show times and tickets!

ATLANTA EAGLE – The Atlanta Eagle, Atlanta's best-known leather bar, is famous for its cavernous dark rooms and shadowy corners. The DJ always spins great music for patrons on the small but lively dance floor.

FYI: The crowd at the Eagle tends to be hard-core, so pretty boys and dolled up drag queens don't really play here. *306 Ponce De Leon Avenue, 404-873-2453, AtlantaEagle.com*

Insider Tip: For late-night cravings, the 24-hour Krispy Kreme donut and coffee shop is right across the street.

BLAKE'S ON THE PARK – Midtown has many gay hot spots, but none is hotter than Blake's on the Park. Blake's originally opened in 1987 at the intersection of 10th Street and Piedmont Road. Since then, Blake's has been one of Midtown's most popular neighborhood gay bars. Recent renovations have improved Blake's and made this "stand and model" zone a more comfortable place to hang out. The drag shows are hysterical, and the crowd couldn't be cuter. *227 10th Street, 404-892-5786, BlakesOnTheParkAtlanta.com*

Insider Tip: Don't miss the Drag Races on Monday night, Drag Gone Wild on Tuesday, Divas Live on Thursday, and Bingo on Friday.

BULLDOGS – Not many of Atlanta's original gay bars from the 1970s are left, but Bulldogs has been open and pouring since 1978. Beware as you approach the large, well-stocked bar—their bartender's reputation for a heavy-handed drink is infamous. Although the spacious dance floor pumps out hip hop and house, if shaking your tail is not your thing you can always claim a pool table. Because of its prime location on Peachtree Street, Bulldogs is convenient to the hotels in the area . . . you'll probably meet a visitor or two, and the back patio is a great place to get to know them even better! *893 Peachtree Street, 404-872-3025, BulldogsBar.com*

play

Insider Tip: Although Bulldogs is well known as a black gay bar, it welcomes everyone (especially if you love hip hop).

BURKHART'S – If you're looking for the old biker bar at Ansley Square, it closed in 1988 and has since been replaced by Burkhart's. It's still not a "strike a pose" bar; this is one of the most unpretentious gay bars in Atlanta. It's a very comfortable place to hang out, have a drink and play some pool if you like. The boys here are approachable and laid-back, and on Sundays the legendary Armorettes (see listing under *Give*) will make you laugh until you can't take it anymore. Other nights you can sing karaoke or even grab a full dinner. *1492-F Piedmont Avenue (Ansley Square), 404-872-4403, Burkharts.com*

Insider Tip: Burkhart's patio sprawls across the entire back side of the bar. It's also intimate enough to allow you step step back and disappear into the shadows if you want.

Did You Know?

Atlanta spans over 6,000 square miles (with over 100 streets named Peachtree) and is host to almost 19 million visitors each year.

CHARLIE BROWN'S CABARET – Charlie Brown has been performing for gay and straight crowds in Atlanta for years. She and the other cast members who perform along with her have been featured on HBO, The Travel Channel, VH1, and TBS. After Atlanta's notorious 24-hour club Backstreet closed (and where her show used to be housed), this queen of queens clawed her way to the top of another marquee bearing her name when Charlie Brown's Cabaret opened at Underground Atlanta in January of 2005. Designed to resemble a New Orleans bordello, this theatre of female impersonation, illusion, and fantasy is an Atlanta standard not to be missed. Come watch the Magnificent 7-Raven, Shawnna Brooks, Heather Daniels, Lena Lust, Lauren LeMasters, Ashley Kruiz and, of course, Charlie Brown herself—Thursday through Saturday at 11 p.m. *Underground Atlanta, 50 Upper Alabama Street, 678-904-4512, CharlieBrownsCabaret.net*

Insider Tip: Since Charlie Brown's Cabaret is located in Underground Atlanta, there's no shortage of bars and restaurants where you can grab a drink, a quick bite, or a full meal before the show.

COMPOUND – Throw on your best designer outfit, jouge your hair, and cough up the cover charge so you too can become one of the beautiful people who flock to Compound. This uber-posh club is situated on the west side of the city in an area that has enjoyed recent rebirth. Compound is actually more of a club complex, with several different bars, buildings, and courtyards to entice you. Past the velvet rope you'll find an outdoor Zen garden complete with rock pathways, bamboo, and a reflecting pool fed by gurgling fountains. Mies van der Rohe couldn't have designed anything more striking than the lounge "MB1" which showcases various DJs and has a great audio and video system along with another full bar. Step out the back door and you'll find another sub-club called "Ride" which includes a huge dance house and 20 flat screens lining the walls (as a well as a super hard-hitting sound system that will definitely put a beat in your

play

brain)! Although the crowd is mostly metrosexual and trendsexual, a fair share of gay boys love to come here and dance too. *1008 Brady Avenue, 404-872-4621, CompoundATL.com*

Insider Tip: Keep your eye out for the private VIP bedroom that includes an all-glass shower for celebrities and VIPs who may start to feel just a little bit dirty. If you can get in, you never know who you might bump into!

EL CHAPARRAL – Ay Papi! El Chaparral is primarily a Latin club—and when we say Latin, we mean *Latin*. Although it's sometimes hard to find someone who speaks perfect English, who cares when the boys are hot, hot, hot! Inside you'll find two bars on either side of an expansive dance floor that pumps out authentic Latin music. You can also just plop down on the pleasant leather couches and enjoy a nice siesta. *2715 Buford Highway, 404-634-3737*

Insider Tip: To appease your hunger after grinding on the dance floor, El Chaparral also offers a small café serving up tacos and burritos late into the night.

ELEVEN50 – One of the first upscale downtown clubs (named for its address), eleven50 is a glorious old theatre that's been turned into a chic nightclub. Along with an inviting dance floor, there are also some great lounge areas around the club and upstairs in the balcony where you can relax after a long night. Eden, the gorgeous outdoor garden and patio, offers a full bar with oversized beds and private cabanas along with a dramatic fountain and sexy lighting. *1150-B Peachtree Street, 404-874-0428, eleven50.com*

Insider Tip: Although the crowd is normally straight, be sure to check out "Thump" on Wednesdays—it's just for the boys.

FUTURE – One of eight new clubs that recently opened in Kenny's Alley in Underground Atlanta, Future is touted as the underground of Underground, where you'll find hardcore dance music along with a cyber-erotic dance area to complete your sensory overload experience. The club is surrounded with high-resolution screens and even has a VIP balcony area for those who are "dressed the part." If you decide to drop in after a late night at the office and don't have time to change, there are even private changing rooms and a lounge where you can get dressed—or undressed! *Underground Atlanta, 50 Upper Alabama Street, 678-904-2457, FutureAtlanta.com*

Insider Tip: Club nights are based on themes of carnal pleasures, like Wednesdays' "FUC" (Future Underground Club) which is reserved strictly for the boys.

HALO – For a "pretty" experience, check in to the Biltmore Hotel's basement for a visit to Halo. Thursday night is boy's night, and you'll find them dressed, pressed and ready to parade. The DJ is always spinning something groovy with a great beat. The lounge is funky and industrial, with stairs leading up to the ceiling, red leather furniture, cool lighting, and a large video screen showing your favorite Bollywood movies. If you like S&M (standing and modeling), then you'll love Halo. *817 West Peachtree Street #100, 404-962-7333 HaloLounge.com*

Insider Tip: Although it's unmarked and a little mysterious in the Biltmore Hotel's basement, Halo isn't too hard to find. Just look for the large bouncer guarding the metal door down the street from Toast (see listing under *Eat: American-Contemporary*).

play

HERETIC – After closing its doors for good, Claire's Chowder House—where your grandma and grandpa probably ate at the buffet for $4.95-later reopened as the Heretic. The inside is very moody, and two bars are located in rooms on either side of the dance floor. The DJ pumps out good music, and everyone dances hard. Sometimes there's a cover charge, but it's usually less than the cost of your grandparent's buffet we mentioned earlier. There's also a back deck that overlooks the free parking lot. Be sure to check out the leather shop, where all types of "gifts" are for sale. *2069 Cheshire Bridge Road, 404-325-3061, HereticAtlanta.com*

Insider Tip: The back hall of the Heretic has a notorious reputation for heavy breathing and a little groaning ... venture there if you dare. Also be prepared for the "dress code" to be enforced. Some nights the only way to get on the dance floor is to rip off your shirt!

HOEDOWNS – "You can't keep a good ho' down!" is Hoedown's motto—this is gay country at its finest. Inside you'll find a huge main bar that's manned by hot (and usually shirtless) bartenders. If you don't know how to two-step, you'll learn fast when someone asks you to dance! The bar patrons are loaded with Southern charm and are famously flirtatious. Don't be thrown for a loop when the crowd begins to linedance to Madonna—just watch and try to pick up the rhythm. Who knows, you might get picked up too! Since Hoedown's was featured in the *Designing Women* reunion special, you may even get to chime in with Julia Sugarbaker when the club's video screen plays her "Night the Lights Went Out in Georgia" speech. *931 Monroe Drive, 404-876-0001, HoeDownsAtlanta.com*

Insider Tip: If you yearn to dance like the boys on the dance floor, Hoedowns offers line-dancing classes. Tuesdays are for beginners and Wednesdays and Thursdays are for those who already know a little somethin'. Visit their Web site or call for more information.

JUNGLE CLUB – The newest addition to the gay Atlanta dance scene, Jungle Club is always filled with shirtless boys dancing away and showing off their washboard abs and perky pecs on the stage and on large dance cubes. The bar is huge and tended by shirtless, perfectly-toned muscle boys. There are also several jungle-themed rooms around the warehouse-sized dance floor where you can sit, chat, or make out if you just can't help yourself. The cover charge is a bit steep on some nights, but definitely worth it for the music, DJs, and dancing. Jungle is the sister club of Red Chair Video Lounge (see listing under *Play*). *2115 Faulkner Road, 404-844-8800, JungleClub.net*

Insider Tip: On the way in, you can pay $25 instead of the usual cover and receive a $25 bar tab in exchange.

KENNY'S ALLEY AT UNDERGROUND ATLANTA – Underground Atlanta has seen many renovations and revamps over the years—though downtown Atlanta's reputation as a haven for crime has been the main problem, scaring off would-be patrons. Recently, however, the city has worked hard to change Underground's image and has saturated the area with police officers. Secure lots offer ample parking. *Underground Atlanta, 50 Upper Alabama Street, 404-523-2311, Underground-Atlanta.com*

Insider Tip: If driving isn't your thing, MARTA's Five Points station directly connects to Underground. This is great for when you want to cruise Kenny's Alley until 4 a.m. with drink in hand!

THE LOFT – One of Atlanta's newest club innovations, the Loft is a 15,000 square foot lounge above EarthLink Live's music complex. Along with oversized sofas, windows overlooking West Peachtree Street, a premium sound system, and a VIP room, the Loft features gay nights along with other themes, events, and performances. *1374 West Peachtree Street (17th Street), Floor 2, 404-885-1365, TheLoftATL.com*

THE MARK ULTRALOUNGE – The Mark Ultralounge overflows with sleek and sexy lines—and the trend-setters who come for the music, dancing, and drinks are sleek and sexy as well. There's a large bar downstairs and a small one upstairs, and both floors have plenty of lounge areas for when you need to rest and relax. The dance floor is located downstairs and belts out hip hop, funk, house, and trance. A custom-designed, state-of-the-art sound and lighting system enhances the mood and heightens the senses. *70 Poplar Street, 678-904-0050, TheMarkAtlanta.com*

MARY'S – There are a few good gay bars outside of Midtown, and Mary's is one of these. A great hole-in-the-wall neighborhood stop, Mary's is known for its karaoke night as well as a bar that's usually packed with an array of alterna-punk guys, hotties sporting tattoos, and well-groomed Gucci-clad boys. And when we say packed, we mean packed! Mary's—which occupies a former notions shop—is long and narrow and lined on one side by a big bar. Upstairs you'll find a nice place to stand and watch the crowd below or play some pool. In the back of the bar and also on the porch there's some good conversational seating. Don't worry about wearing the latest couture, since attitude is the only thing missing at Mary's. *1287 Glenwood Avenue, 404-624-4411*

Insider Tip: For music lovers, Mary's DJ plays great Brit-pop, alterna-punk, and American pop mixed with 80s favorites.

THE MASQUERADE – Housed in a turn-of-the-century mill building, The Masquerade has featured rock concerts and special events since 1989. A mixed crowd is normally in attendance, so the amount of ATLANTAboys present will depend on the show. Thursday nights welcome those 18 and up with alternative dance hits from the 80s and 90s. *695 North Avenue, 404-577-8178, Masq.com*

Insider Tip: Saturdays are reserved for ATLANTAboys, thanks to Volume Productions' (see VolumeProductionz.com) "Werk Hard" night.

METRO – Once a seedy gay bar from the old days, the Metro has become a little more vanilla after a recent re-vamp. The club is now a melting pot for every type of gay guy the city has to offer. There's often a heavy Latin crowd, and on some nights the DJ spins the latest Latin dance music. Friday and Monday drag shows are always full of energy, and Wicked Wednesdays are, well … wicked! *1080 Peachtree Street, 404-874-9869, TheMetroAtlanta.com*

MISS Q'S – Amsterdam Avenue is home to Amsterdam Walk, which offers fantastic shopping and bars—including Miss Q's. You'll find high ceilings, pool tables, air hockey tables, dart boards, cushy couches, and a bar with ample seating. If you show up in thongs (we mean flip-flops, not underwear), shorts, and a T-shirt—and check the attitude at the door—you'll fit right in. It's a great neighborhood hang-out for gay boys and lesbians. Come to play a few rounds of pool or have a few rounds of drinks . . . it's all one big family here! *560 Amsterdam Avenue, 404-875-6255*

NEW ORDER – New Order is for a more mature crowd. The entrance is behind Ansley Mall—look for a small awning over the door. One of Atlanta's first gay bars (it was once called "El Matador" in the 1970s), New Order welcomes older gentlemen who like to tell tales of days gone by. It's not the non-stop party you'll find elsewhere, but the conversation is good, as are the drinks—which are reasonable and potent! *1544 Piedmont Road (Ansley Mall), 404-874-8247*

THE OSCAR'S – If you love to sing along with your favorite divas, you're in for an entertaining night at the Oscar's video bar. There are screens everywhere—there's even a big video wall at the end of the bar. One of the more popular theme nights is Show Tunes night when you can sing along with Liza, Barbra, and their showbiz sisters. Other nights the DJ plays all of our favorites—from Donna Summer to J-Lo. The in-the-round bar makes it easy to flirt with the cute guy across from you while you wait for him to send a drink your way. *1510-C Piedmont Avenue (Ansley Square), 404-874-7748*

Insider Tip: Although you may find a bit of "Atlantatude" at The Oscar's, it usually disappears once the boys start singing along to Dolly Parton's "Hard Candy Christmas."

PHOENIX – The Phoenix has been called the "best gay redneck bar in Atlanta." Located on Ponce De Leon Avenue, it still holds a reputation from a time when the surrounding area was very seedy. Like any neighborhood bar, the pool table and the bar stools are often occupied by regulars. Patrons generally show up in whatever they threw on in the morning, just to watch TV or catch up on the latest gossip. Busier times at the bar make it a good place to meet "Mr. Right Now," but perhaps not "Mr. Right." *567 Ponce De Leon Avenue, 404-892-7871*

Insider Tip: Don't bother trying to show off your new designer outfit—the Phoenix regulars couldn't care less!

RED CHAIR VIDEO LOUNGE – This huge upscale video lounge and restaurant is a popular favorite among both the young crowd and older crowd. Stop by for a full lunch and dinner menu and enjoy a weekly movie screening or viewing party for your favorite television shows like *Will and Grace* and *Desperate Housewives*. Or simply sip a drink in the smoke-free bar while you watch your favorite music videos on six large video screens. On Saturday nights the restaurant becomes a dance floor that carries on the party from 2:30 a.m. until the sun comes up. *550-C Amsterdam Avenue, 404-870-0532, RedChairAtlanta.com*

Insider Tip: Saturday night at Red Chair starts out as Ladies' Night. So if you'd rather be with the boys, stop by Jungle Club first (see listing under *Play*), then head back to Red Chair after 2:30 a.m. for "Insomnia."

SWINGING RICHARDS – This fully nude male strip club (which you won't find in Miami, Las Vegas or L.A.) features some of the hottest dirty dancers in the Bible Belt. With over

65 performers, Swinging Richards is the largest all-male strip club in the U.S. Large is indeed a good word to describe this place—as well as the dancer's ... um ... "richards." The mirrored stage features every type of guy to tickle your fancy, from built centerfold models to hot frat boys to barely legal twinks. Although the drink prices are a bit steep, they're huge and almost as strong as jet-fuel. Bring a group of friends and plenty of single bills for tips and you'll have a blast. *1715 Northside Drive, 404-355-6787*

Insider Tip: Although they have more dancers on the weekends, Tuesday nights are your best bet if you're looking for cute local boys!

WETBAR – If you think they'll like Thursday's weekly college night, bring your friends to WETbar and take a body shot off one of their in-house frat boys or just sit back and watch a good old-fashioned game of lube wrestling! Some nights you'll even find scantily-clad dancers with perfectly toned bodies and cute smiles dancing on the bar. The bars, one downstairs and one upstairs, draw quite a crowd. The upstairs space opens onto a large patio with a sweeping view of Midtown and downtown—and a bird's-eye view of the men waiting to get in! *960 Spring Street, 404-745-9494, WetBarAtlanta.com*

WOOF'S ON PIEDMONT – In an unassuming shopping center you'll find Woof's, Atlanta's only gay sports bar. TVs tuned to ESPN, college pennants, team banners, and beer signs—for most of us this sounds like our worst nightmare. But if you love sports—or the men who play them—you'll love Woof's. The men packed wall-to-wall inside are a little on the bearish side. Grab a chair, a beer, some greasy bar food, and watch the game. *2424 Piedmont Road, 404-869-9422, WoofsAtlanta.com*

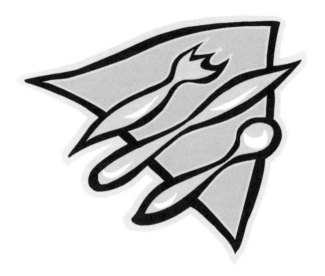

In This Chapter

24–Hour Diners • American-Contemporary • American-Traditional • Barbeque (BBQ) • Bistros • Coffee Shops • Continental • Cuban • Delis • Dessert • Hamburger Joints • Italian • Japanese/Sushi • Mediterranean • Mexican • Noodle Houses • Pizza • Seafood • Southern • Southwestern • Spanish/Tapas • Specialty Grocery Stores • Steakhouses • Thai • Vietnamese

eat

Atlanta offers one of the best selections of restaurants in the country, with several rated in the top ten in the United States. Whether you're looking for a 24–hour diner after a long night at a club or a celebrity chef's showcase establishment, you'll find it here in Atlanta. A tip of 15% to 20% is customary, and if the restaurant is upscale, make sure you call ahead to make a reservation.

$$$$	Over $40
$$$	$30 - $39
$$	$20 - $29
$	$10 - $19
¢	Under $10

* Prices are per person for a main course dinner.

24–HOUR DINERS

$ MAJESTIC DINER – Truly an American landmark, the Majestic Diner's neon sign has been shining since 1929. The crowd tends to be mixed–from Little Five Points punks to neighborhood families to in-the-know ATLANTAboys. Pork chops, burgers, meats with three vegetables, and breakfast standards are all available 24/7. *Plaza Shopping Center, 1031 Ponce De Leon Avenue (North Highland Avenue), 404-875-0276*

Insider Tip: Seating is available at booths, tables, or the counter any time, so the Majestic makes a great stop for munchies after a night out.

¢ **WAFFLE HOUSE** – Waffle House is the mother of all 24–hour diners in Atlanta. The yellow sign is always on and the coffee is always pouring at this eatery where breakfast is the mainstay. There's one on every corner to quench your thirst and satisfy your appetite. *2264 Cheshire Bridge Road, 404-634-9414, WaffleHouse.com*

Insider Tip: The Cheshire Bridge location is just down the road from late night hot spots Jungle and the Heretic (see listings under *Play*).

AMERICAN-CONTEMPORARY

$$$$ **BACCHANALIA** – Bacchanalia is one of Atlanta's hottest restaurants. Originally located in a Buckhead cottage, it moved to its current Westside location in 1993 to serve contemporary American cuisine that's light but flavorful. Bacchanalia is plush and elegant without feeling overly formal and affords diners sweeping views of the Midtown skyline. Try the Maine lobster appetizer and the wood-grilled California squab.
Westside Marketplace, 1198 Howell Mill Road (between 14th Street & Huff Road), 404-365-0410, StarProvisions.com

Insider Tip: For dessert try the sheep's milk yogurt panna cotta with lavender-infused organic strawberries . . . yum!

$$$ **BAZZAAR** – Located in the corner of the Fox Theatre (see listing under *Watch*), this upscale European restaurant and lounge serves modern American cuisine in a

sleek setting that's perfect for conversation and cocktails. A live DJ spins tunes Thursday through Saturday. *654 Peachtree Street (Ponce De Leon Avenue), 404-885-7505, BazzaarAtlanta.com.*

Insider Tip: You'll find complimentary parking across the street at the Georgian Terrace Hotel (see listing under *Stay*) . . . just be sure to get your parking ticket validated!

$$ **EINSTEIN'S** – A part of the Metrotainment Café family, Einstein's is a huge supporter of the gay community. Einstein's has been a fixture of Midtown since 1991, offering new and innovative dining in a warm and cozy environment. Occupying three of Atlanta's classic 1920s bungalows, the restaurant has evolved over the years into a beautifully posh and hip hang-out. The bar and lounge are in the first bungalow which is tricked out with funky fixtures, a fireplace lounge, and a granite-topped bar that seats up to 50 people. The drink menu is also impressive, featuring a tempting array of martinis. The second bungalow offers booth seating and group dining for up to 100 guests. If the weather is warm, angle for a table or the beautiful patio. The grilled salmon is great, and the homemade desserts are incredible—be sure to check out the daily specials! *1077 Juniper Street NE (12th Street NE), 404-876-7925, EinsteinsAtlanta.com*

Insider Tip: You must try Einstein's Sunday brunch along with one of their famous—or infamous—Bloody Marys!

$$$ **ONE. MIDTOWN KITCHEN** – Everyone from late-night hipsters to middle-aged matrons and gay gourmands knows ONE.Midtown Kitchen is a one-of-a-kind restaurant occupying a renovated warehouse with a view of Piedmont Park and the Atlanta skyline. One features al

fresco dining, an 80–foot curved counter, an open kitchen, and serenely understated décor. Considering this restaurant's hip factor, prices are fantastic—and so is the food. The uncomplicated yet delicious cuisine is made with the freshest local produce. Famed menu samplings include the hanger steak on parmesan-herb fries with red-wine shallot sauce and an amazing lamb rib dish baked in a honey, chipotle, and soy sauce marinade. *559 Dutch Valley Road, 404–892–4111, OneMidtownKitchen.com*

Insider Tip: Call ahead for preferred seating so you can slide on in and eat your heart out!

$$$ **PLEASANT PEASANT** – A staple of Atlanta fine dining since the mid-1970s, the Pleasant Peasant is still casual enough to welcome you even if you show up in your jeans. Since many theatre-goers stop in on their way to the Fox Theatre (see listing under *Watch*) for a show, a tux or business attire is welcome also. Exposed brick layered with art and mirrors enhances and relaxes the surroundings. Be sure to check out the dazzling wine list! *555 Peachtree Street (Linden Avenue), 404–874–3223, ThePeasantRestaurants.com*

Insider Tip: The plumb pork is to die for, and the French onion soup is divine!

$$ **RATHBURN'S RESTAURANT** – Rathburn's is dramatic: a loft space with exposed brick, a beautiful bar, and a long wine list. While the vibe is casual, reservations are recommended. Some of chef Kevin Rathburn's favorite dishes are equally popular with the patrons—the Maine lobster soft taco, sea scallop benedict, and the vegetarian-friendly butternut squash tortellini. *Stove Works Lofts, 112 Krog Street #R, 404–524–8280, RathburnsRestaurant.com*

eat

$$$ **SPICE** – Riding a new wave of fine dining, Spice is located in an old Atlanta home that has turned into an opulent culinary laboratory. Modern art and photography adorn the walls, and colorful tropical aquariums enchant the eye. Be sure to try seasonal selections that are prepared to the highest standards. *793 Juniper Street (5th Street), 404-875-4242, SpiceRestaurant.com*

$$$$ **SUN DIAL RESTAURANT, BAR & VIEW** – Standing at 723 feet, the Sun Dial Restaurant is a dining experience that you have to see to believe. The Westin Peachtree Plaza (see listing under *Stay*) in downtown Atlanta is home to this tri-level restaurant and bar. Take the 85-second ride to the top of the tower in one of two glass elevators to kick off this feast for the eyes. The dining area revolves giving an unobstructed, 360-degree view of Atlanta's skyline. It's truly breathtaking on clear nights. Try to break away from the view and actually savor the food or a selection from the wine list ... not to mention the specialty desserts! *Westin Peachtree Plaza, 210 Peachtree Street, Floor 71 (Garnett Street), 404-589-7506, SunDialRestaurant.com*

Insider Tip: If you take a trip to the bathroom, try not to get too lost on the way back ... your table probably won't be where you left it!

$$$ **TOAST** – Specializing in simple, creative American fare, Toast looks like it belongs in South Beach rather than Atlanta—but we're not complaining! Since it's adjacent to Halo (which is gay on Thursday nights—see listing under *Play*), make a reservation for dinner then walk next door for the rest of your evening out on the town. *817 West Peachtree Street, Suite E-125 (Behind the Biltmore at 6th Street and Cypress Street), 404-815-9243, ToastRestaurant.com*

Insider Tip: Be sure to try their signature Toasty sandwich!

$$$ TWO.URBAN LICKS – Featuring "live fire cooking" (in a 14-foot open-fire rotisserie), gravity drawn wines, and a kitchen-in-the-round, TWO.Urban Licks—the sister restaurant of ONE. midtown kitchen (see listing under *Eat: American-Contemporary*)—is an eye-opening and tongue-grabbing experience. The open-fire rotisserie is the largest in the country and uses a refurbished 1895 Forge to slow-cook meat and fish. Diners can watch food preparations in the kitchen while they catch the vibe in a high-energy environment in this renovated warehouse that's surprisingly inviting and undeniably hip. *820 Ralph McGill Boulevard, 404-522-4622, TwoUrbanLicks.com*

Insider Tip: Look for the 42 stainless steel barrels of wine that greet you at the door. They're drawn by gravity and served as half glass, full glass, and mini/full thief. They're also temperature controlled to protect against oxidation

$$ VICKERY'S BAR & GRILL – Vickery's has been in Atlanta since 1983. The restaurant is named after Margaret Vickery, who ran an antique shop in the house. Rumor has it that she and Margaret Mitchell used to be good friends, and that some of *Gone With the Wind* was written in the house when Mitchell would visit. Vickery's serves hamburgers and steaks, but the real treat is the New Southern Cuisine with a Cuban and Caribbean twist. *1106 Crescent Avenue (12th Street), 404-881-1106, VickerysBarAndGrill.com*

Insider Tip: Vickery's Low Country grits with crab meat and andouille sausage are perfection. Diners also love the Caribbean jerk chicken and the black bean cakes.

$ WOLFGANG PUCK EXPRESS – Best known as the celebrity chef of Spago in Beverly Hills, Wolfgang Puck has brought his delicious creations to Atlanta in the form of "fast gourmet." You can dine in for the full experience or take it home with you to watch your favorite TV show. You must try one of Wolfgang's signature pizzas, but if you want something a little more "fork and knife," try any of the reasonably-priced entrees with the garlic mashed potatoes or the herbed French fries. Quick, easy, and oh so yummy! *Brookhaven Village Shopping Plaza, 1745 Peachtree Street #H-J (25th Street), 404-815-1500, WolfgangPuck.com*

AMERICAN-TRADITIONAL

$ JOE'S ON JUNIPER – The patio at Joe's is definitely one of the best places to see and be seen in gay Atlanta. Food favorites include the Angus burgers, sandwiches, and flaming (or mild) buffalo wings. With a full bar offering $5 martinis every day, weekend "blunch" (their version of brunch with beer), over 30 beers on draft (plus over 100 bottled ones), and quick and sassy service, you simply can't go wrong. On Monday, Tuesday, and Thursday nights you can strain your brain with trivia. Grab a pitcher of beer and a group of friends and have a blast, but get there early for a table. There's a more limited menu after hours, but it's still fabulous! *1049 Juniper Street, 404-875-6634, JoesAtlanta.com*

Insider Tip: Since Joe's is part of the Metrotainment Cafe family, they serve tempting Metrotainment Bakery (see listing under *Eat: Dessert*) desserts—a must-taste!

$$ MURPHY'S – Your love of good food will take you to this popular neighborhood hangout. Founded in 1980 in a bungalow basement by Tom Murphy, Murphy's has since moved to one of the best-known intersections in the city: Virginia Avenue and North Highland Avenue, the heart of the shopping and dining district known as Virginia-Highlands. Rafters and exposed brick preserve the original basement feel, while skillful lighting creates a comfortable and airy setting. The food is delightfully unpredictable and inventive, and there's a wine list with over 300 selections. Popular dishes include sautéed crab cakes with vegetable escabeche and a delicious salmon BLT with roasted tomatoes and smoked bacon. *997 Virginia Avenue (North Highland Avenue), 404-872-0904, MurphysVH.com*

Insider Tip: The weekend brunch is a favorite, but be prepared to wait—they don't take reservations for this meal.

$ THUMBS UP – This funky-fresh eatery is very popular—expect to wait for up to an hour—but the energetic and friendly wait staff and scrumptious food makes it worth the wait. Made from scratch, the meals are hearty and delicious. They even whip up their own whole-wheat biscuits and jam every day! It's a hot spot for the who's who of Atlanta at breakfast, with everyone from lawyers and business professionals to political figures sitting down for a good dose of Southern cookin'. You may even get to trade condiments with a local politician or celebrity. *573 Edgewood Avenue (Bradley Street), 404-223-0690*

Insider Tip: ATLANTAboy suggests the caramel apple French toast or the Southwestern egg wrap. Even though they say "no substitutions," they just might accommodate you if you ask nice!

$$ WEST EGG CAFÉ – The Westside of Atlanta is home to one of the city's latest renaissance movements—new homes, apartments, and dining options seem to open every day. The West Egg Café is a stand-out, serving breakfast and lunch daily in an old converted garage with a great fireplace and plush lounge area. For all your surfing needs there's free wireless Internet access and a bottomless cup of coffee to help keep you perky. *1168-A Howell Mill Road, 404-872-3973, WestEggCafe.com*

Insider Tip: ATLANTAboy recommends the fried green tomato wrap and the Coca-Cola cupcakes. And make sure to ask for their daily specials!

BARBEQUE (BBQ)

$ **DUSTY'S BARBEQUE** – People have been eating heartily at Dusty's BBQ since 1981. A tender and juicy barbeque dinner attracts both local celebrities and ATLANTAboys to this cabin-like eating house. Along with traditional barbeque sauce flavors, you'll also find their "Sizzlin" signature sauce. It's good enough to buy by the gallon—and you can! *1815 Briarcliff Road (Clifton Road), 404-320-6284, Dustys.com*

$ **FAT MATT'S RIB SHACK** – Fat Matt's started serving up blues and their award-winning BBQ in 1990. This cash-only establishment is small but the food packs a bang. The shack may fill up fast—remember that patience is a virtue and that tables do turn over quickly. Don't worry though, the BBQ will make the wait worthwhile. *1811 Piedmont Avenue, 404-607-1622, FatMattsRibShack.com*

Insider Tip: If you can't wait for the crowd to disperse, try Fat Matt's Chicken Shack next door for true Southern fried chicken and seafood.

BISTROS / DELIS

$ ALON'S BAKERY & MARKET – A cross between a European bistro and a New York deli, Alon's offers an array of homemade pastries, breads, sandwiches, and cakes. Beware: it's all good ... *really* good. You've been warned, so let your sweet tooth run wild, skip the diet for a day, and stock up. *1394 North Highland Avenue, 404-872-6000, Alons.com*

Insider Tip: Try the tiramisu or the homemade cookie dough—just don't tell anyone you heard about it from us!

CHINESE

$ LITTLE BANGKOK – You'll find affordably tasty Thai and Chinese food at this wee restaurant appropriately named Little Bangkok. The lunch specials are all delicious and run about $5. The dining room is a little more tightly packed for dinner, but the food's just as tasty. *2225 Cheshire Bride Road (Woodland Avenue), 404-315-1530*

$$$ SILK – Along with steak, lobster, and sushi, Silk offers an amazing ambiance with four waterfalls, a German limestone flooring with embedded ancient fossils, and a private alcove draped in what else ... silk! *919 Peachtree Street (The Metropolis Building), 678-705-8888, SilkRestaurant.com*

Insider Tip: Order a "Purple Rain" martini, made with Japanese/Korean spirits and garnished with purple basil!

COFFEE SHOPS

APRÈS DIEM
(See listing in *Eat: Continental*)

CAFÉ INTERMEZZO
(See listing below in *Eat: Dessert*)

$ JOE'S EAST ATLANTA COFFEE SHOP – This neighborhood dive serves up hot coffee and delicious desserts. Several cushy mismatched sofas and homey rugs adorn the inside, which also boasts a ceiling painted to resemble the dome of the Sistine Chapel. The surroundings are calm and laid-back, as are the many patrons. It's a mix of urban hipsters, tattooed artists and ATLANTAboys. If work is still pulling at your pants leg, they also have free wireless Internet access. *510 Flat Shoals Avenue, 404-521-1122*

Insider Tip: The cake slices are massive—plenty for two people to share!

OUTWRITE BOOKSTORE & COFFEEHOUSE
(See listing in *Shop*)

CONTINENTAL

$$$$ ABBEY – Set in a former Midtown church (circa 1915), the Abbey's dramatic setting offers a unique dining experience. Featuring stained-glass windows, vaulted ceilings, and servers dressed as monks, the Abbey also accommodates large parties (private dining rooms available). *163 Ponce De Leon Avenue (Piedmont Avenue), 404-876-8532, TheAbbeyRestaurant.com.*

Insider Tip: ATLANTAboy loves the Abbey's impressive wine list!

$$ APRÈS DIEM – Tucked away in the back of the Midtown Promenade Shopping Center sits Après Diem. You won't see it from the street, but it's there. This restaurant and coffeehouse welcomes an eclectic crowd with a sexy ambience quite suitable for a date or even a relaxed night with friends. You can either wait for a seat or walk straight through to the back room where you'll find plush sofas and chairs arranged into small conversation areas. A delicious brunch is offered on Saturday and Sunday mornings—don't think twice about getting a bagel with lox and cream cheese—it's the best. When there's not a live DJ spinning, you'll at least hear acid jazz or something with a funky beat being piped in. Aprés Diem boasts great food and fantastic coffees plus a full drink and dessert bar that lasts long into the night. *Midtown Promenade Shopping Center, 931 Monroe Drive (Virginia Avenue), 404-872-3333, ApresDiem.com*

Insider Tip: Take a seat on one of the sofas in the back room (there's no wait if one is available) and order the Café Affogoto (ice cream with a shot of espresso.)

Did You Know?

Atlanta was the fifth city to be the capital of the state of Georgia. First there were Savannah, Augusta, Louisville, and Milledgeville.

CUBAN

$ LAS PALMERAS – Off the beaten path, Las Palmeras offers some of the best jerk chicken you'll find outside of Miami or Havana. Since it's located right in the middle of a residential neighborhood, be on the lookout or you'll miss it. It's well worth the trip, and the food is ridiculously low priced. *366 5th Street (Durant Place), 404-872-0846*

Insider Tip: Be sure to call ahead—they tend to keep odd hours.

DESSERT

$$ **CAFÉ INTERMEZZO** – One of the best places for coffee, conversation, and dessert, Café Intermezzo is a longtime Atlanta favorite. If you've always wanted to learn French or Italian, just visit the bathroom, where you'll hear the language tapes you remember from high school. Along with a sunny back patio that's covered if it's rainy, there's also a dark and sexy dining room to savor their decadent treats. *1845 Peachtree Road, 404-355-0411, CafeIntermezzo.com*

$$$ **METROTAINMENT BAKERY** – Metrotainment Cafés is responsible for the success of many restaurants in Atlanta and has been a longtime supporter of the gay community. All of the desserts served in their restaurants come from one place: the Metrotainment Bakery. Their fabulous cakes, pies, and sweets are made with the finest ingredients and are baked fresh daily. The bakery originally started out on Juniper Street, but within a year it had grown too big for its bunt pans! Future plans include adding a retail area and café so you can sit for a while and enjoy a slice or two of delicious dessert. *691 14th Street, 404-873-6307, MetroBakery.com*

Insider Tip: ATLANTAboy knows from experience that all of Metrotainment Bakery's chocolate concoctions are so decadent, they give Southern Decadence in New Orleans a run for its money!

¢ **JAKE'S ICE CREAM** – Although Jake's serves food as well, this relaxing Midtown location is best known for its homemade ice cream. Flavors such as Choco Nana Chip Joyscream and Chocolate Slap Yo Mamma make it virtually irresistible. Our favorite is the coffee ice cream with chunks of Krispy Kreme donuts. *970 Piedmont Avenue (10th Street), 404-685-3101; 676 Highland Avenue (Sampson Street), 404-523-1830; 1540 North Decatur Road, 404-371-0890 JakesIceCream.com*

Insider Tip: If you don't do dairy, Jake's also serves a variety of dairy-free soy flavors as well as homemade sorbets.

HAMBURGER JOINTS

$ **THE VORTEX BAR & GRILL** – The Vortex Bar and Grill in Little Five Points was founded in 1992 by three siblings, and the Peachtree Street location is its sister restaurant. The walls are plastered with an eclectic collection of memorabilia—from autographed celebrity photos to entire human skeletons and vintage advertising. If you're looking for the "perfect burger," your search is over—the Vortex's burgers are nationally recognized as some of the best. The menu even instructs diners on how to behave (there's a strict "No Idiot Policy"). The beer selection features a wide array of labels and tastes, and the "booze" selection is nothing to shake a stick at either. This watering hole is no corporate-controlled cookie-cutter bar—the Vortex sets its own rules. *878 Peachtree Street (between 7th & 8th Streets), 404-875-1667, TheVortexBarAndGrill.com*

> ### *Did You Know?*
>
> The Varsity Restaurant has served more Coca-Cola than any other dining establishment in the world. It provides nearly 3 million servings of Coke a year. *61 North Avenue, 404-881-1706; 1085 Lindbergh Drive, 404-261-8843, TheVaristy.com.*

ITALIAN

$$ BARAONDA – Established in 1999, Baraonda is an authentic brick-oven pizzeria and café Italiano located on the corner of Peachtree and 3rd Streets. Choices range from the tame "Margherita" mozzarella and basil pizza to the more spunky "Salmone" pizza with smoked salmon and parsley. Baraonda also offers traditional pizzas, calzones, and pastas along with a superb wine selection. The menu changes all the time, and there's a separate dinner menu for Sundays. *710 Peachtree Street (3rd Street), 404-879-9962, BaraondaAtlanta.com*

Insider Tip: You'll find complimentary parking across the street at the Georgian Terrace Hotel (see listing under *Stay*) . . . just be sure to get your parking ticket validated!

$ Figo Pasta – Figo Pasta is a small, cozy café that lets you build your own dishes from a list of over 15 varieties of pasta and 11 fresh sauces. The sauce recipes come from the owner's grandmother—and the food is authentic down to the last noodle. Simply place your order at the counter and find a seat and sit down. A server will bring your meal as soon as it's piping hot. It's quick and easy for dining in or for take-out. Milanese youth use the word "Figo" to refer to something that they love and appreciate to describe a great new idea or concept, which is a perfect name for this place! *1210 Howell Mill Road (Huff Road), 404-351-3700; 1170-B Collier Road (Defoors Ferry Road), 404-351-9667, FigoPasta.com*

Insider Tip: If the line is out the door, don't worry—it moves quickly and the experience is well worth the wait!

$$$$ **FLOATAWAY CAFÉ** – The Floataway Café is located on the outskirts of Midtown, close to Emory University. Most of the nearby buildings were originally transfer warehouses or loading docks for railroad cargo and have since been renovated to make room for galleries and Internet businesses. *Southern Voice* (see listing under *Read*), Atlanta's gay newspaper, calls this area home. Active railroad tracks lie 100 yards from the restaurant, listen and you'll hear the train while you sit on the open-air courtyard. The seasonal cuisine is influenced by country French, Mediterranean, and Italian flavors. This sibling of Bacchanalia's (see listing under *Eat: American-Contemporary*), offers wood-grilled skirt steak and tasty wood-fired pizzas. *1123 Zonolite Road, Suite 1-5, 404-892-1414, StarProvisions.com/Float*

Insider Tip: This one's a bit hard to find, so look for the Briarcliff Animal Clinic at the start of Zonolite Road. Then follow the road to the right by the railroad tracks to reach the café.

$ **LITTLE AZIO** – Little Azio isn't so little when it comes to taste. The kitchen serves up tasty pizzas, pasta, and panini in a contemporary Italian setting. You can also build your own dish from a list of toppings. The location is close to many other gay hot spots, and it's a great place to stop for picnic food on your way to Piedmont Park. *903 Peachtree Street, 404-876-7771, LittleAzio.com*

Insider Tip: Also check out Little Azio's big brother Azio, which is located downtown. *229 Peachtree Street, 404-222-0808, AzioDowntown.com.*

$ **OSTERIA 832** – Virginia-Highlands plays host to many funky fun eateries. Osteria 832 is one of those, known for its Italian pizzas and pastas, although it's not just a pizza joint. It's name comes from the street address and the Italian word for "tavern." The restaurant and crowd are both cool, casual, and a bit on the noisy side, but you won't notice while you're tearing into of their fantastic thin-crust pizzas or tasty pasta dishes. *832 North Highland Avenue (3 blocks north of Ponce De Leon Avenue), 404-897-1414, Osteria832.com*

JAPANESE / SUSHI

$$ **NICKIEMOTO'S** – Nickiemoto's touts what they call "Sushi Art," and if you like sushi, you'll love this restaurant. Take a seat outside for a great view of all the boys on their way to Piedmont Park or Blake's (see listing under *Play*). On any given night you may even spot a drag queen floating by, which means it's either time for the drag show at Blake's or it's Monday night at Nickiemoto's, which means Drag-A-Maki! *990 Piedmont Avenue (10th Street), 404-253-2010*

Insider Tip: For the best experience at Drag-A-Maki, ATLANTAboy recommends taking a group of people, and don't forget to make a reservation! The best drag shows here spill into the parking lot and stop traffic . . . literally!

$ **RU SAN'S** – Ru San's boasts a great dollar menu and an all-you-can-eat sushi bar that doesn't end until 3 p.m. When the evening crowd starts to pour in, Ru San's becomes a loud "sushi" party where the staff hollers, customers laugh, and the music pumps. Call ahead if you don't want to wait. *Ansley Square, 1529 Piedmont Road (Monroe Drive), 404-875-7042*

Insider Tip: Try ordering the Sake-Bomb. It's a blast to watch and even more fun to drink!

MEDITERRANEAN

$$$$ **ENO** – Are you on the prowl for a neighborhood restaurant and wine bar? Eno, a small but lively sidewalk café and restaurant, allows visitors to taste and learn about a wide variety of food, wines, and cheeses. This Old World restaurant boasts a wine list that emphasizes selections from Italy, Spain, and Greece. Over 80 wines are available as tasters (275 wines are available by the bottle) along with 15 varieties of champagne. The European-Mediterranean features savory specialties like braised veal Osso Bucco, seared Maine diver scallops and Provencal onion tart with olives. The restaurant is also adorned with artwork from Gallerie Timothy Tew. *800 Peachtree Street (5th Street), 404-685-3191, Eno-Atlanta.com*

Insider Tip: Try Eno's wine-tasting on Tuesday nights!

$$ **GILBERT'S MEDITERRANEAN CAFÉ** – Next door to Blake's on the Park (see listing under *Play*) is Gilbert's. Al-

though the restaurant is cozy and softly lit for a romantic evening, if you stick around long enough the bar can get pretty wild! Mediterranean food like cilantro and mango-encrusted trout, lamb tenderloin, and baklava are made with fresh ingredients and prepared to order. *219 10th Street (Piedmont Avenue), 404-872-8012, GilbertsCafe.com*

Insider Tip: You can watch the girls belly-dance every other Wednesday, and the boys belly dance on Tuesdays!

$$ THE GRAPE – The Grape is a sophisticated wine bar, and its other half, The Grape Seller, is a fun and welcoming store offering a wide variety of wines and helpful service. The company has even copyrighted a 10-point classification system that makes it easy to find (and taste) what you're looking for. The wine bar is a cozy and enticing gathering place with both indoor and outdoor seating. More than 120 wines by the bottle, glass, or half glass tempt you to try before you buy and complimenting the wines is a selection of specially prepared gourmet fare. *999 Peachtree Street, 678-309-9463, YourGrape.com*

Insider Tip: Don't miss the wine-tasting on Saturdays!

MEXICAN

$ NUEVO LAREDO CANTINA – Nuevo Laredo Cantina opened in 1992 to serve the area's local lunch crowd and has since become one of Atlanta's hottest Mexican restaurants. Chance Evans opened the restaurant to serve authentic home-cooked Mexican fare to Atlanta, and he continues to do so with great success. Heavily laden with awards and accolades, this is not your typical

Mexican restaurant. The inside is cozy and bedecked with hand-picked items imported directly from Mexico. Crowds are always plentiful—while there's sometimes a wait, it's well worth it. *1495 Chattahoochee Avenue (between Collier & Howell Mill Roads), 404-352-9009, NuevoLaredoCantina.com*

Insider Tip: Be sure to try the Margaritas. Have just one and you'll stay all night!

$$ **UNCLE JULIO'S CASA GRANDE** – Uncle Julio's Casa Grande is an old adobe building that has been renovated with bright colors and neon lights. You can't miss it! Inside there are mismatched tiles, velvet paintings, and wagon-wheel light fixtures. There's also plenty of space for large groups. The service is fast and fun and the food is tasty . . . a far cry from the Americanized Mexican fast food atrocities we've become accustomed to. *1860 Peachtree Road (Collier Road), 404-350-6767, UncleJulios.com*

Insider Tip: Although the crowd at Casa Grande is normally straight, on Fridays the ATLANTAboys take over!

¢ **WILLY'S MEXICANA GRILL** – Right next to the 14th Street entrance to Piedmont Park you'll find Willy's which occupies the old American Legion Building. Willy's is a great place to see and be seen by all the ATLANTAboys going to and from the park. The burritos and quesadillas are so good that a crowd is usually lined up out the front door waiting to get in. And don't forget—they also serve beer and margaritas. *1071-C Piedmont Avenue (12th Street), 404-249-9054, WillysMexicanaGrill.com*

$$ **ZOCALO** – Taken from the Mexican word for "plinth" (a large stone), Zocalo does not serve your average Mexi-

can cuisine. The food is spicy, fresh, and totally justifies the short wait you may have to endure. *187 10th Street (Piedmont Avenue), 404-249-7576, Zo-Ca-Lo.com*

Insider Tip: Zocalo is located right down the street from Blake's on the Park (see listing under *Play*) . . . head over for a drink and a drag show after your meal!

NOODLE HOUSES

$ **DOC CHEY'S** – This comfortably funky noodle house at two gay-friendly locations serves food with inspiration from China, Japan, Korea, Thailand, and Vietnam. The large portions make this a favorite choice for anyone on a budget. *Highland Walk, 1424 North Highland Avenue (University Avenue), 404-888-0777; Emory Village, 1556 North Decatur Road, 404-378-8188, DocCheysNoodleHouse.com*

Insider Tip: Doc Chey's became famous among ATLANTAboys after Danny Roberts (the openly gay star of *Real World: New Orleans*) proclaimed it his favorite Atlanta restaurant. His boyfriend brought some of his favorite dishes to him in one of the series' most memorable episodes.

$ **NOODLE** – Deep red murals accent the walls in this sleek and sexy restaurant where patrons sit at a long sparkling bar to enjoy delicious noodle bowls. The tables at Noodle are cozy and comfortable and there are two-seat booths that provide a more intimate dining experience for you and a friend. There's also patio seating available. The noodle bowls are the best, and the appetizers are certainly . . . well . . . appetizing! *903 Peachtree Street (8th Street), 404-685-3010, NoodleHouse.net*

PIZZA

$ Fellini's Pizza – Although pizza by the slice is a foreign concept in the South, it's slowly catching on. Fellini's Pizza sells their pies by the slice as well as whole pizzas, calzones, salads, and much more. You can either build your own sizeable slice or pick from some of Fellini's preset favorites. Several locations adorn the city, so there's always one just around the corner. *909 Ponce De Leon Avenue (Linwood Avenue), 404-873-3088; 2809 Peachtree Road (Rumson Road), 404-266-0082; 1634 McLendon Avenue (Clifton Road), 404-687-9190; 1991 Howell Mill Road (Collier Road), 404-352-0799; 4429 Roswell Road (Wieuca Road), 404-303-8248*

Insider Tip: If you're not sure what to get, try Fellini's "Special Pizza," which has a little bit of everything tossed on top.

$ GRANT CENTRAL PIZZA – Grant Central Pizza takes its name and decor from Grand Central Station in New York City and its location in Grant Park. You can build your own pizza by the slice or the whole pie. Both locations are neighborhood hangouts, where you'll find a large beer selection as well. Aside from pizzas, you can enjoy Italian fare such as calzones, pastas, and salads. *451 Cherokee Avenue (Glenwood Avenue), 404-523-8900* and *1279 Glenwood Avenue (Flat Shoals Road), 404-627-0007*

SEAFOOD

$$$ FISHMONGER – Fishmonger is located on the gay block of Midtown near the intersection of Piedmont Road and

10th Street across from Outwrite Bookstore (see listing under *Shop*). The fish is absolutely fresh and comes from all over the world, including delicious sun fish from Hawaii that's shipped in daily. Fishmonger's culinary wizards whip up around six specials per day! *980 Piedmont Avenue, 404-881-8889, FishmongerSeafoodGrill.com*

Insider Tip: The sun fish are farm-raised in Hawaii and fed only macadamia nuts, which give them a nutty, sweet flavor—definitely worth a try!

$ SIX FEET UNDER – Named for its location near the historic Oakland Cemetery, Six Feet Under is laid back, frou-frou-free and includes a well-stocked bar where you can order beer and other libations. Pleasant and efficient servers welcome everyone from artists and musicians to "family," families, and all their friends. Outside you'll find a rooftop deck with glorious skyline views of the city and cemetary. *415 Memorial Drive (Oakland Avenue), 404-523-6664, SixFeetUnderAtlanta.com*

Insider Tip: Be sure to taste the baked parmesan-crusted grouper!

SOUTHERN

$$ AGNES & MURIEL'S – This tasty stop is quite a hit with ATLANTAboys—perhaps because the fare reminds us of mom's cooking. Agnes & Muriel's—named for the owners' mothers—serves "food you only *wish* your mom cooked" along with many Southern favorites like fried green tomatoes—which was made famous by the book and movie of the same name. Along with a selection of wine and beer and sangria, they also pour sparkling Mimosas, Bloody Marys, and Poinsettias at brunch. Don't try to steal the recipes from the kitchen—just buy the cookbook and be sure not to skip out without trying a slice of the red velvet cake. It's as good as mom makes . . . literally! *1514 Monroe Drive (Piedmont Avenue), 404-885-1000, AgnesAndMuriels.com*

Insider Tip: ATLANTAboy recommends the tangy and pleasing Louisiana BBQ shrimp or the juicy Coca-Cola BBQ ribs. Be sure to call ahead for preferred seating!

$ **COLONNADE** – The Colonnade is set in one of Midtown's most "interesting" stretches of Cheshire Bridge Road. Nestled between the Heretic (see listing under *Play*), Inserection (an adult novelty store—see listing under *Shop*) and a few antique shops, the Colonnade caters to a clientele that includes everyone from leather lovers to old women. In fact, this bastion of Southern food and cheap cocktails has been nicknamed "The Gay and Gray." Serving up traditional Southern lunches—meat and three veggies—and dinners since 1927, the Colonnade is a place your grandparents would love. *1879 Cheshire Bridge Road (between Lavista Road and Piedmont Avenue), 404-874-5642*

Insider Tip: If you do decide to visit with the whole family, you'll be relieved to know that there's a full bar!

$ **FLYING BISCUIT** – This Atlanta favorite on the corner of 10th Street and Piedmont Road offers more than just biscuits. The fare is health-conscious Southern food (no, not an oxymoron) made with all-natural, organic ingredients.

Dine inside and enjoy the hip décor or dine on the corner patio and watch ATLANTAboys walk by on their way to the park. Breakfast—one of the best in Midtown—is served all day every day, and if you want to cook your own tasty vittles at home you can even buy the cookbook! *1001 Piedmont Avenue (10th Street), 404-874-8887; 1655 McLendon Avenue (Clifton Road), 404-687-8888, FlyingBiscuit.com*

Insider Tip: The "Meatloaf and Pudge" is an old family recipe!

$$ **MARY MAC'S TEA ROOM** – One of the last "tea rooms" in Atlanta, Mary Mac's has been serving up traditional Southern cooking since 1945. The tea room seats over 350 and serves an average of 2000 meals each day. The recipes haven't changed since Margaret Lupo opened the restaurant, and everything is cooked from scratch. Mary Mac's serves it up seven days a week, including Sunday brunch. *224 Ponce De Leon Avenue (Piedmont Avenue), 404-876-1800, MaryMacs.com*

Insider Tip: Try the meatloaf. And if you've never had pot likkar, just ask and they'll give you a bowl for free!

SOUTHWESTERN

$$ **AGAVE** – Agave offers an extensive menu with entrees like spicy Diablo crawfish pasta and sunburned strip steak. The wine selection is worth a try, as well as the very impressive tequila menu that boasts over 80 types of

tequila. Plenty of mixed drinks are served as well—including the best margaritas in Atlanta. Smooth, tangy, and always amazing. For groups of up to 100 people there is a "chef's menu." At $25–$30 per person ($50 with wine or tequila), it's a great deal! *242 Boulevard SE (Carroll Street), 404-588-0006, AgaveRestaurant.com*

Insider Tip: ATLANTAboy recommends Agave's sashimi pan-seared tuna along with the creamy mashed potatoes. And of course a margarita—or three!

$ **FROG'S CANTINA** – Frog's Cantina serves up lots of Southwestern yummies with a full bar and a shaded patio. The beer selection is good, but the fish tacos are even better! It's a great stop before or after a stroll through Piedmont Park, which is just a block away. *Midtown Promenade, 931 Monroe Drive, 404-607-9967*

Insider Tip: Don't leave your car in the free lot to go to the park—it will get booted or towed!

$ **MOE'S SOUTHWEST GRILL** – Welcome to Moe's! This brightly lit, colorful restaurant serves food made with the freshest ingredients. Nothing is ever frozen, and all the meats are marinated and grilled using no animal fat or lard. This location is near L.A. Fitness (see listing under *Sweat*), and ATLANTAboys come to get dinner or a protein-filled snack after their workout. *Ansley Mall, 1544 Piedmont Avenue (Monroe Drive), 404-879-9663, Moes.com*

$ **TAQUERIA DEL SOL** – Taqueria del Sol is well known for both its tasty tacos and mouth-watering margaritas. All locations are bright and inviting and stay busy for both lunch and dinner. It's "semi-self-serve" with a wait staff—order your food and drinks at the counter, find a table and have a few sips of your margarita and while you wait for your food. Although there are other entrees, the tacos are a specialty and they're only about $2 each. *1200-B Howell Mill Road (Huff Road), 404-352-5812, TaqueriaDelSol.com*

Insider Tip: Both the fish and Memphis (BBQ) tacos are delicious.

SPANISH / TAPAS

$$ **ECLIPSE DI LUNA** – Eclipse di Luna isn't your typical watering hole. This evening eatery in a design district of antique shops, decorator studios, and furniture show rooms is the last stop on Miami Circle just off Piedmont Road. A wild Spanish-influenced tapas menu is served up in an artsy, remodeled warehouse where live Latin music flows through the restaurant and onto the patio. Get there early or be prepared to wait—there is plenty of free parking. For a calm lunch alone, a private party, or a large dinner, Eclipse scores high. *764 Miami Circle NE (Piedmont Road), 404-846-0449, EclipseDiLuna.com*

Insider Tip: Eclipse also offers wireless Internet service.

$$ **LOCA LUNA** – Sandwiched between the Armory (see listing under *Play*) and the now-closed Backstreet nightclub, Loca Luna serves up small plates of fantastic tapas. The large koi-filled fountain and tropical plants create an

indoor Euro-oasis. During pleasant weather, the roof opens to reveal an enchanting view of the moon and stars. Live entertainment varies each night—sometimes you might even catch a little salsa dancing! *836 Juniper Street (between 6th and 7th Streets), 404-875-4494, Loca-Luna.com*

Insider Tip: The fish tacos are scrumptious, and the "Patatas Bravas" are spicy and tasty!

$$ **RED CHAIR RESTAURANT** – Red Chair is a double-edged sword: half the club operates as a full-service tapas bar and restaurant (with burgers also!) during dining hours, and a full-fledged nightclub in the evening (see listing under Play). *550-C Amsterdam Avenue, 404-870-0532, RedChairAtlanta.com*

Insider Tip: Check out Red Chair's weekly events that include 'Dinner and a Movie' nights and viewing parties for our favorite TV shows.

SPECIALTY GROCERY STORES

SEVANANDA – Sevananda is one of the largest consumer-owned cooperatives in the Southeast. (A co-op is owned by the people who shop there). Providing fresh organic produce, healthy natural foods, herbs, and household products to the community has been Sevananda's mission since it opened its doors, empowering the community to improve its health and well-being. *467 Moreland Avenue, 404-681-2831, Sevananda.com*

STAR PROVISIONS – Have you ever gone to dinner and been so moved by the food that you ask, "Where can we buy this amazing foie gras?" or "Could you possibly order us some truffles?" Well diners at Bacchanalia (see listing under *Eat: American-Contemporary*) did, so the owners created Star Provisions. If you've ever wanted to walk into a restaurant's pantry or kitchen and pick up what you want to take home, this is it! The carefully organized store is a chef's paradise—you'll find everything from restaurant-quality cookware and gadgets to seasonal tableware and linens. Star Provisions has everything you need to turn your kitchen into your own little Bacchanalia. *1198 Howell Mill Road, 404-365-0410, StarProvisions.com.*

WHOLE FOODS MARKET – Located in the heart of Midtown on Ponce De Leon Avenue, Whole Foods Market is the grocery store of choice for those seeking a huge selection of the freshest organic and conventional fruits and vegetables, baked goods, cheeses and wines. *650 Ponce De Leon Avenue, 404-853-1681, WholeFoodsMarket.com*

Insider Tip: Shopping while hungry is allowed here—there are food sample stations throughout the store.

Did You Know?

The Whole Foods Midtown location was once home to the Atlanta Crackers minor league baseball team. In 1907, the Ponce De Leon Ball Park opened next to a magnolia tree that marked a home run for the batters who reached it. The stadium burned to the ground in 1923, but the famed magnolia tree still stands behind the Whole Foods store today!

STEAKHOUSES

$$ COWTIPPERS – Cowtippers opened its doors in 1993 and has since become a huge supporter of the gay community as well as an Atlanta landmark. This casual eatery is home to usual steakhouse fare as well as a few of their own creations. They serve up thick char-grilled steaks, fresh seafood, juicy chicken, and gigantic burgers. Tantalizing homemade desserts and 25 types of margaritas brought to your table by an attractive and fun staff. The enormous outdoor patio always packed during the spring and summer months. *1600 Piedmont Avenue (Monroe Road), 404-874-3751, CowTippersAtlanta.com*

Insider Tip: ATLANTAboy suggests driving by and checking out the scene. You may even see a rugby team holding a car wash fundraiser in the parking lot—shirtless!

THAI

$$ THAI CHILI – Thai me up and sit me down! Thai Chili serves Thai-inspired dishes under the direction of owner and Head Chef Robert Khankiew. Intimate lighting, artfully hung pictures, and distinctive statues create an inviting atmosphere. Thai Chili has racked up many awards and accolades for its delectable cuisine, which will beckon you back for more. *Briarvista Shopping Center, 2169 Briarcliff Road (Lavista Road), 404-315-6750; Colony Square, 1197 Peachtree Street #517 (14th Street), 404-875-2275, ThaiChiliCuisine.com*

eat

VIETNAMESE

$$ **NAM** – A romantic dinner spot tucked away in the Midtown Promenade shopping center, Nam features flowing curtains, gorgeous waiters in beautiful red chemises, and an eclectic menu of contemporary Vietnamese food. The intimately sexy scene makes Nam a perfect spot for dinner. *931 Monroe Drive (Midtown Promenade, Ponce De Leon Avenue), 404-541-9997, NamRestaurant.com*

Insider Tip: Try the "Claypot Chicken," then head next door to the Midtown Art Cinema to catch the latest gay-themed indie film.

Big Gay Supper Club

Want to experience a variety of restaurants and meet new friends at the same time? Check out the Big Gay Supper Club. This social group hosts a monthly four course dinner at one of Atlanta's hottest restaurants for around 100 people. Visit their Web site to find out where the next event will be held.
BigGaySupperClub.com

In This Chapter

Antique Stores • Boutiques • Malls • Shops • Storefronts

shop

From unique boutiques to large shopping malls, there are a multitude of places to shop in Atlanta. Whether you're on the prowl for a bargain-priced pair of shoes, a pricy new wardrobe, or even a new fountain for your yard, you'll find it at one of the gay-friendly shops below.

ATLANTA WATER GARDENS – The Atlanta Water Gardens is a full-service retail gardening center. The store's specialty is pond installation and maintenance—you'll find anything and everything you'll ever need under one roof. Koi fish, plants, pond chemicals, liners, pumps and filters, statues, garden art—the list goes on and on. For smaller interests, AWG stocks table-top fountains and gift items for any occasion. The whole shebang is set up inside, with full ponds featuring live fish and plants on display. It's a beautiful and enchanting place simply to walk around and get lost in. *2165 Cheshire Bridge Road, 404-235-0739, AtlantaWaterGarens.com*

Insider Tip: In November, Atlanta Water Gardens hosts their anniversary party with wine, cheese, and music.

BED DOWN – Looking for luxurious linens? Check out Bed Down, which has everything you need for a good night's sleep. Custom-designed beds and sheets as well as bedroom furniture are on display along with throws, tables, mirrors, sofas, and more. *504 Amsterdam Avenue, 404-872-3696, BedDown.com*

BELVEDERE – Belvedere is a design store that emphasizes elegant mid-20th century furniture and accessories. Pieces range from antique French 40s, vintage classic, modern and contemporary designs all with a focus on beauty, comfort, and function. Designers include well-known icons and also some who are just now being discovered. You'll also find art selections by Jonathan Adler, Chris Fitzmiller, Philip Crangi, and more. *1200 Howell Mill, 404-352-1942, BelvedereInc.com*

> ## *Did You Know?*
>
> In 1942, Hartsfield-Jackson International Airport, once named Candler Field, set a record of 1,700 takeoffs and landings in one day, earning the title "the nation's busiest airport." In 1946 the name was changed to Atlanta Municipal, then to the William B. Hartsfield Atlanta International Airport in July of 1971. After the death of former mayor Maynard Jackson in 2003, the airport became the Hartsfield-Jackson International-Airport. Today it's known as "the world's busiest passenger airport," serving over 76 million passengers each year.

BOY NEXT DOOR – Boy Next Door has been selling its wares to the community in the same location since 1980. The store is always full to the brim with ATLANTAboys trying on form-fitting clothes and stylish shoes (that can't be found in a mall) in a barely-there changing area. Local celebrities, actors, and dancers shop here as well as many visiting porn stars. Be sure to check out their great selection of music and accessories as well. *1447 Piedmont Road, 404-873-2664*

Insider Tip: Boy Next Door also features one of the hottest underwear and swimwear selections in the Southeast!

BRUSHSTROKES – A one-stop shop for gays and lesbians, Brushstrokes offers everything from pride paraphernalia to gay porn to novelties, gifts, cards, stationery, and T-shirts. Looking for that hard-to-find import CD? You'll find it in their movie and music section, which is enormous. And as we all know, size does matter! Brushstrokes offers something for everyone, and the staff is as sweet as cherry-flavored lube! *1510 Piedmont Avenue #J, 404-876-6567, BrushstrokesAtlanta.com*

Insider Tip: Brushstrokes also features a large selection of adult videos, magazines, and toys.

BUNGALOW – Atlanta's Craftsman Bungalow-style homes are a hot commodity right now, and the store Bungalow is just as hot. Named by CitySearch.com as one of the top five home furnishing stores in Atlanta, the shop carries everything from furniture and bedding to bath lighting and home accessories. Martha Stewart would love the "back room" filled with luxurious linens, and she would be giddy to learn that the sister-store across the street stocks her namesake products. Rumor has it that Usher, a well-known Atlantan who appreciates the finer things in life, shops here often. *1198 Howell Mill Road, 404-367-8522*

BY DESIGN – By Design is one of those places where everyone goes to buy something for their house or condo. Whether it's an entire collection of furniture or just a vase, By Design is definitely "in" in Atlanta. The international collection is sold at low direct-import prices, offering modern-contemporary furniture and retro-modern pieces by Belair and other designers! *1747 Cheshire Bridge Road, 404-607-9098, ByDesignFurniture.com*

CANTONI – Visiting Cantoni is a dazzling experience for your senses as well as for your home. The store is large, featuring stylishly cool furniture, lighting, and accessories that are all clean and minimalist. They also offer everything from shaggy floor coverings to wild art and home accessories. Don't miss their unique lighting selection which—as a certain hotel heiress would say—is "hot." *1011 Monroe Drive, 404-881-8111, Cantoni.com*

CAPULETS – Capulets is an extension of Brushstrokes' (see listing under *Shop*) pride and gift selection. Along with rainbow and pride items, they carry unique gifts, incense, stuffed animals, candles, posters, and for all you dirrrty boys—bath products. *1510-J Piedmont Avenue, 404-876-9003, BrushstrokesAtlanta.com/Capulets*

COOKS WAREHOUSE – The name explains it all, but Cook's Warehouse is much more than just a store. While you can buy every kind of spatula imaginable, you can also learn how to become a gourmet cook through classes taught by professional chefs. Cookbooks line the walls next to gadgets that make life easier while you try to grate cheeses or grind coffee beans. It's a great place to get lost in for an hour before you go home and whip up a delicious meal. *549 Amsterdam Avenue, 404-815-4993, CooksWareHouse.com*

ED'S GOURMET RECORDS – A trip to ED's Gourmet Records is a trip to heaven for DJs and dance music fans alike. The store's selection consists mainly of dance music, but they also carry lots of chill lounge music and vinyl. ED's is one of the best DJ stores in the South, with DJ Abel, Mike B, Andre Perry, Lydia Prim, Joe Guthreaux, Ted Patterson, and even RuPaul attesting to that. *1875 Piedmont Road, 404-876-1557, EDsRecords.com*

FRENCH KISS – A business that bloomed out of the trunk of a car, French Kiss has blossomed into a chic designer store full of European clothing for men and women. You'll find pieces from Dolce & Gabbanna, BCBG, Versace, Ben Sherman, and Sergia Davila among others. And if you're desperate to try a new look, French Kiss has always got something up their sleeve. *900 Peachtree Street, Suite #100B, 404-815-8727, FrenchKissATL.com*

HABERSHAM GARDENS – For an unmatched selection of indoor and outdoor plants, garden art, and accessories visit Habersham Gardens. This nursery stocks everything for your garden and offers fresh cut flowers for your house. Whether your jade plant is dropping leaves or your Southern Indian Hybrid Azaleas are droopy, they'll give you the expert and friendly advice you need to perk them up! *2067 Manchester Street, 404-873-2484, HabershamGardens.com*

Insider Tip: If you're looking for landscape services, Habersham has a landscaping division with 27 years experience. Just ask—they'll tell you about it.

INSERECTION – Looking for a little Kristen Bjorn or Falcon action? You'll find it at Inserection, Atlanta's top choice for adult novelties. Here you'll find every video and sex toy for both gay and straight adults that you could ever want. Although locations are scattered throughout metro Atlanta, the Cheshire Bridge location has the best gay selection as well as a large gay clientele. *1739 Cheshire Bridge Road, 404-875-9200, Inserection.com*

INTAGLIA – This home collection was designed in a neutral palette to allow pieces to easily blend into any space, either as an addition or to begin the process of dressing a room. Enjoy their fancy yet unpretentious showroom, and be sure to check out their selection of accessories, frames, rugs, and art. The store is mainly contemporary, and for the designs, the prices are quite reasonable. *533 Amsterdam Avenue, 404-607-9750, IntagliaHome.com*

INTERIOR DIMENSIONS – This showroom is consistently different; every visit will reveal new pieces in an ever-changing environment. More than just furniture, Interior Dimensions also offers framed artwork that's new and fresh along with bold rugs and lighting options from calm to crazy. The staff can provide design services for the bedroom or the entire house. *915 Peachtree Street (The Metropolis), 404-870-2133, ID-Home.com*

JUNKMAN'S DAUGHTER – Do you love Target stores? Do you love punk? How would you feel about a Punk Rock Target? Well Atlanta's got one! Junkman's Daughter is the original funky-punk store in Little Five Points. The store offers rock-star pants, graphic tees, wild shoes, and all kids of little do-dads and knick-knacks. The behemoth storefront looks like a giant tattoo. Don't plan on a short trip—it can take a while to make one lap through! *464 Moreland Avenue, 404-577-3188*

Insider Tip: If you should happen to visit Athens, Georgia, check out their sibling store, *Junkman's Daughter's Brother, 458 East Clayton Street, 706-543-4454*

LENOX SQUARE – Atlanta's best-known shopping mall houses a food court, movie theater, plus the following stores and more: Abercrombie & Fitch, American Eagle, Aveda Lifestyle Store, Banana Republic, Bloomingdales, Cartier, Club Monaco, Crate & Barrel, Gap, Guess?, J. Crew, Kenneth Cole, Kiehl's, Lacoste, Louis Vuitton, The Mac Store, Neiman Marcus, Polo by Ralph Lauren, Pottery Barn, Macy's, Storehouse, Urban Outfitters, Versace Jeans Couture, Vidal Sassoon, Williams-Sonoma and more. *404-233-6767, 3393 Peachtree Road, LenoxSquare.com*

LIGNE ROSET – Ligne Roset was established in 1860, when the company made brentwood walking sticks. Since then, it has become a multinational contemporary furniture company with a team of talented and innovative designers. These designers work with playful and unconventional materials—including glass, ceramic, and plastic. From concept to final piece, all designs of furniture and accessories are closely observed and approved by the designers and managers. These unique and chic designs are too posh to pass up! *805 Peachtree Street, 404-881-0500, Ligne-Roset-USA.com*

METROPOLITAN DELUXE – Mix a little city chic with modern sleek and toss in some flowers, cards, and furniture and you've got Metropolitan Deluxe. Check out the fragrant flowers that are fresh every day as well as the wide selection of aromatic candles. They also offer a large variety of stationary and cards—some funny, some serious, and some racy for just the right moment. Plenty of funky accessories for the home and office fill the shelves. Downstairs is the furniture showroom with contemporary beds, dressers, light fixtures, and more. *1034 North Highland Avenue, 404-892-9337, MetropolitanDeluxe.com*

NO MAS PRODUCTIONS – No Mas Productions is a distinctive furniture and home accessories store on Atlanta's Westside. The place overflows with hand-forged furnishings and accessories that can't be found anywhere else in the city. No Mas carries nothing that is mass produced–in other words, "no mass productions." They work directly with over 100 artisans in Central Mexico to create unique hand-carved tables and armoires, dramatic chandeliers, and beautiful hand-painted tiles. The bathroom even has a hand-painted toilet! The demand for garden and outdoor items led No Mas to open Bodega Gardens, where you'll find everything from small fountains to large garden sculptures. *790 Huff Road, 404-350-0907, NoMasProductions.com*

OUTWRITE BOOKSTORE & COFFEEHOUSE – Outwrite Bookstore and Coffeehouse is more than just coffee and books–it's a place where a huge cross-section of the community can bump into each other and hang out. The store was founded in 1993 and moved to its present location in 1996, occupying a space that had housed an old disco called Red Square. Along with coffee drinks to keep you awake, the café also sells delicious sandwiches and scrumptious desserts. Along with a large variety of gay-genre books, the store also sells CDs, DVDs, magazines and gifts. Outwrite often hosts book signings by celebrity authors like Carson Kressley, Tammy Faye Messner, Kyan Douglas, Chastity Bono, and Christopher Rice. *991 Piedmont Avenue, 404-607-0082, OutwriteBooks.com*

PARIS ON PONCE – Paris on Ponce is an antique-hunting experience unlike any other. When they opened their doors in the late 1990s, the owners wanted to create an engaging store where people could come to browse. The complex comprises three buildings and the mood is the

shop

reminiscent of your grandparent's attic. There are plenty of unique and hard-to-find antique items including beds, mirrors, magazines, and dolls. Also be sure to check out the lush theater space, Moulin Rouge, which is available for parties and private events. *716 Ponce de Leon, 404-249-9965, ParisOnPonce.com*

PHIPPS PLAZA – Atlanta's most upscale shopping mall houses a food court, movie theater, plus the following stores and more: A|X Armani Exchange, Barneys New York, Gap, Giorgio Armani, Gucci, Niketown, Nordstrom, Parisian, Saks Fifth Avenue, Versace, and Williams-Sonoma, *3500 Peachtree Road, 404-262-0992, PhippsPlaza.com*

POSTER HUT / SCREAM BOUTIQUE – The Poster Hut is your local gay department store, featuring quality merchandise at good prices. They offer cards, gifts, frames, novelties, jewelry, and accessories for both the body and the home. Scream Boutique—the clothing store—offers everything from hip and trendy crop tops and low-rise pants to leather vests and harnesses. *2175 Cheshire Bridge Road, 404-633-7491*

RETROMODERN – One of only two stores in the U.S. that carries designs by Alessi (along with his complete line of accessories), Retromodern also offers mid-century modern designs by Knoll, Herman Miller, and Kartell. Check out their unique line of designer flatware, serving pieces, kitchen utensils, and lighting fixtures. *805 Peachtree Street, 404-724-0093, Retromodern.com*

SHOEMAKER'S WAREHOUSE – The Shoemaker's Warehouse would send the ladies from *Sex and the City* into a tailspin. The list of designers featured here ranges from Kenneth Cole and BCBG to Sketchers and Steve

Madden—all at incredibly low prices. After shopping here, you may want to go back into your closet and never come out! *500-A Amsterdam Avenue, 404-881-9301, ShoeMakersWarehouse.com*

SKATE ESCAPE – Skate Escape is sure to "get you rolling." Roller blades, inline skates, bicycles, and accessories are all available for rent and or purchase at Skate Escape. It's located directly across the street from Piedmont Park, which makes it an easy stop before an afternoon stroll. They can also provide you with lessons on how to stop in your new skates without having to grab the nearest stationary object. Of course, with so many cute boys at the park to grab a hold of, you may find that you don't really want lessons after all! *1086 Piedmont Avenue, 404-892-1292, SkateEscape.com*

SPACE – Space offers the very best in upscale European contemporary furniture and accessories. Here you'll find designers such as Cassina, Minotti, Molteni, and Venini. Space also features architecturally inspired pieces by Philippe Starck, classics such as Le Corbusier, Mies Van der Rohe, Frank Lloyd Wright, and more. A fun space to shop, you'll find champagne, bottled water, wine, and soda available along with the best in chill groove music. They also offer space-planning through the eyes of some truly talented designers. *800-A Peachtree Street, 404-228-4600, SpaceModern.com*

TWELVE – Twelve is a two-part package deal with separate buildings just a block away from each other. At 976 Piedmont you'll find a gift shop that's one-stop-shopping for fabulous gifts, music, art, and jewelry. They sell work from local artists and act as an "underground" music source for imports and unreleased CDs. The shop at 1000

shop

Piedmont is a full-service floral shop. Here you'll find everything from traditional houseplants to brilliant floral designs. Stop in for an individual arrangement or enlist the designer's talents for an entire event. *976 Piedmont Avenue, 404-897-5511, 1000 Piedmont Avenue, 404-541-2357*

UNIVERSAL GEAR – Whenever you feel like shedding your old look for a decadent new designer outfit, head over to Universal Gear. This contemporary men's retail store always features the latest fashions from urban designers such as G-Star, Diesel, Adidas and more. Don't miss their fashion shows, which feature hot underwear models. *935 Peachtree Street (The Metropolis), 404-872-5700, UniversalGear.com*

YES. A HOME STORE – Yes, YES is all about you! This home furnishings and accents store was designed with both the contemporary and classic in mind, carrying an eclectic mix of hard-to-find gifts, furniture, original art, home accents, and lighting to meet your every need. *921-B Peachtree Street (The Metropolis), 404-733-5909, Yes1Mc.com*

Did You Know?

Alanta has more shopping center space per capita than any other city except Chicago. You would have to visit three shopping centers a day to see all of them in a year! It's also home to the fourteenth largest mall in the nation—the Mall of Georgia.

In This Chapter

Art Museums • Ballet • Cabarets • Cinemas • Concerts • Opera • Playhouses • Symphonies • Theatres

watch

With its historically rich cultural scene, Atlanta has no shortage of options when you'd like to spend a night at the theatre. It's no wonder that Elton John premiered his Tony-winning musical *Aida* in Atlanta. Whether you'd like to take in a play, an opera, a musical, or a concert, you're bound to find what you're looking for at one of the theatres below.

14TH STREET PLAYHOUSE – The 14th Street Playhouse is part of the Woodruff Arts Center and houses three stages. The Mainstage seats 400, Stage 2 seats 200, and Stage 3 accommodates an audience of 90. With many different theatrical companies performing here, there's a wide variety of experiences you can enjoy. The 14th Street Playhouse recently hosted the play *My Boyfriend the Stripper*, starring gay porn über-star Matthew Rush and *Real World: Miami* alum Dan Renzi. *173 14th Street, 404-733-4754, Woodruff-Arts.org*

7 STAGES – Founded in 1979 by two theater lovers, 7 Stages started out with a mission: "To create a haven for artists and audiences to address the social, political, and spiritual issues in their daily lives." Originally a 65-seat theatrical outfit in an old storefront, 7 Stages has grown to fill a renovated 1920s movie house. The main stage seats 200, and the smaller theater seats 90. The shows staged here tend to be edgy . . . they even took a risk hosting *10 Naked Men,* who were indeed . . . naked! *1105 Euclid Avenue, 404-523-7647, 7Stages.org*

ACTOR'S EXPRESS – Actor's Express is housed in the King Plow Arts Center, a 1902 plow factory that has been converted into artist studios, galleries, offices, and a custom-designed 120–seat theater. Actor's Express is home to an adventurous non-Equity troupe that pushes the boundaries of traditional theater. Many regional debuts have taken place here and many original plays have premiered here as well. *King Plow Arts Center, 887 West Marietta Street, Suite J-107, 404–875–1606, Actors-Express.com.*

AGATHA'S MYSTERY THEATRE – Zoinks, Scooby-Doo–it's murder mystery night at Agatha's Mystery Theatre! Serving a five-course meal during a comedy murder mystery can take some time, so be prepared to devote three full hours for this one. The theater here is original, but its not quite a traditional theatrical performance. The dining room is the stage, and every member of the audience is invited to have a small part in the production. *693 Peachtree Street, Info Line: 404–875–1610, Box Office & Main Line: 404–875–4321, Agathas.com*

ALLIANCE THEATRE – Founded in 1968, the Alliance Theatre is one of the nation's largest regional theater complexes and is part of the Woodruff Arts Center. It's also one of the nation's only regional theatres that produces professionally staged works for both adults and children. The complex features an 800–seat proscenium-thrust stage and a 200–seat black-box studio. *1280 Peachtree Street, 404–733–5000, AllianceTheatre.org*

Insider Tip: In 1998, Elton John chose the Alliance Theater to premiere his and Tim Rice's production *Elaborate Lives: The Legend of Aida*. The show evolved over the course of its Atlanta run and eventually became the hit musical *Aida* on Broadway.

ANSLEY PARK PLAYHOUSE – The Ansley Park Playhouse is the uptown sister to the Peachtree Playhouse (see listing in *Watch*). Opened in 2002 by playwrights John Gibson and Anthony Morris, the theatre seats 139 and is located in the Peachtree Pointe Building. Ansley Park Playhouse is the new home of the longest-running theatrical production in Atlanta history, *Peachtree Battle*. *1545 Peachtree Street, 404-875-1193, AnsleyParkPlayhouse.com*

ATLANTA BALLET – From its humble beginnings in a garage in 1929, the Atlanta Ballet has become a company that exemplifies the spirit that enlivens the city of Atlanta. As one of the nation's premiere ballet companies, the Atlanta Ballet has long been recognized for its innovative dance. They are also a diverse group, representing a large cross-section of the city. *Performances held at: Fox Theatre, 660 Peachtree Street, 404-873-5811, AtlantaBallet.com*

ATLANTA GAY MEN'S CHORUS – For 24 years, the Atlanta Gay Men's Chorus has been committed to the time-honored tradition of quality male choral music performances while shedding a positive light on the gay and lesbian community. The chorus has blossomed from a small singing group to a full choir of over 150 singing members. They also donate their time and performances to other community organizations and are a joy to hear. *Performances held at: Ferst Center for the Arts, 349 Ferst Drive (Georgia Tech), 404-320-1030, AGMChorus.org*

Insider Tip: The Atlanta Gay Men's Chorus performs an annual Christmas concert that brings in families of all definitions, and the colorful and up-beat Pride concert is not to be missed!

ATLANTA OPERA – Looking for a night at the opera? Atlanta has just the place for you—the Atlanta Opera. Having won many awards, the Opera sets high standards for their productions and strives to educate the community about the art form through services and programs. There are four main stage productions during the season as well as many lectures and educational programs. *Performances held at: Atlanta Civic Center, 395 Piedmont Avenue, 404-881-8885, AtlantaOpera.org*

ATLANTA SYMPHONY ORCHESTRA – The Atlanta Symphony Orchestra first performed in 1945 as a small youth group and has since become an impressive, Grammy-winning, and world-renowned American orchestra. *Performances held at: The Woodruff Arts Center, 1280 Peachtree Street, 404-733-4900, AtlantaSymphony.org*

Insider Tip: See the Atlanta Symphony Orchestra (ASO) in one of its many free concerts during their Free Parks Series, which is performed in parks across the city—including two at Piedmont Park.

THE BOISFEUILLET JONES ATLANTA CIVIC CENTER – One of the largest theaters in the Southeast, the Atlanta Civic Center is also one of the most versatile. It plays host to everything from Broadway plays, theatrical produc-

In This Chapter

Attractions • Gardens • Historic Sites • Museums–Tours • Zoos

PushPush encourages artists to do just that. *121 New Street, 404-377-6332, PushPushTheater.com*

WHOLE WORLD THEATRE – Whole World Theatre was founded in 1994 by David Webster and modeled on the workshops he taught. The improv group values acting, character, and atmosphere more highly than cheap laughs and is devoted to expanding and making advancements in improve theater. *1214 Spring Street, 404-817-0880, WholeWorldTheatre.com*

Did You Know?

Writer Alan Ball wrote the movie *American Beauty* and created the HBO series *Six Feet Under* based on his experiences growing up in Marietta.

visit

If the clubs and bars have worn you out and you'd like to get a little bit more culture out of Atlanta, there are plenty of places where you can do just that. Many of the tours, exhibits, and attractions throughout the city teach the history of Atlanta and allow you to go behind the scenes for a look at how our world-famous corporations like Coca-Cola and CNN operate.

ATLANTA HISTORY CENTER – The Atlanta History Center is located on 133 acres of land in the heart of Buckhead. Showcasing one of the Southeast's largest history museums, a research library, two historic houses and a series of gardens, the center has also just added its fourth signature collection called *Down the Fairway with Bobby Jones* about the world-famous golfer. *130 West Paces Ferry Road, 404-814-4000, AtlantaHistoryCenter.com*

ATLANTA BOTANICAL GARDEN – The Atlanta Botanical Garden features 15 acres of outdoor display gardens, including a high-elevation house, a tropical display house, and a center for education and conservation. The Dorothy Chapman Fuqua Conservatory houses rare and endangered plants from around the world. *1345 Piedmont Avenue, 404-876-5859, AtlantaBotanicalGarden.org*

Insider Tip: During the evening, you can purchase gourmet food, wine, and cheese to create a relaxing (or romantic) escape.

ATLANTA CYCLORAMA – At the Atlanta Cyclorama you'll find the world's largest oil painting, "The Battle of Atlanta." It's a "moving" experience, as you sit in the auditorium and listen to a narrative about the battle while the nine thousand-pound, 358 foot by 42 foot painting revolves around you. *800 Cherokee Avenue, 404-624-1071, BCAtlanta.com*

Insider Tip: The Atlanta Cyclorama is located right next to Zoo Atlanta (see listing under *Visit*), so you can do both in the same day!

CNN CENTER STUDIO TOUR – Your trip to Atlanta wouldn't be complete without a tour of CNN Center. On the CNN Studio Tour, you'll go behind the scenes to learn how the news is covered, twenty-four hours a day! Atlanta is the main hub of CNN, so you never know which hottie anchor you may run into! *190 Marietta Street, 404-827-2300, CNN.com/StudioTour*

Insider Tip: The best place to park is the Centennial Parking Deck on the corner of Centennial Olympic Park Drive and Marietta Street. Save your CNN Tour ticket stub to get a discount on your parking ticket!

FERNBANK MUSEUM OF NATURAL HISTORY – Home to dinosaurs, fossils, artifacts, and even an IMAX Theater, the Fernbank Museum of Natural History is a must if you love science. Its latest permanent exhibition, "Giants of the Mesozoic," showcases the world's largest dinosaurs. *767 Clifton Road, 404-929-6300, Fernbank.edu*

Insider Tip: Check out the neighboring Fernbank Science Center, home of Atlanta's planetarium and observatory. You won't find these stars in *Us Weekly*! *156 Heaton Park Drive, 678-874-7102.*

FERNBANK SCIENCE CENTER & OBSERVATORY – Part of the Fernbank Museum, the Science Center is open every Thursday and Friday night year round (weather permitting). The Fernbank Observatory is a great way to watch the stars (and we're not talking about Britney, Brad, or J-Lo)! *56 Heaton Park Drive, 678-874-7102, FSC.Fernbank.edu*

THE FOX THEATRE – The "Fabulous Fox" opened on Christmas Day in 1929 and is one of the few remaining movie palaces from the 1920s. Take a tour of the Fox and you'll go deep inside the catacombs of Middle Eastern and Egyptian architecture to learn about the inspiration behind the Egyptian Ballroom, the Grand Salon, and the Spanish Room. The tour meets in the Fox Theatre Arcade. *660 Peachtree Street, 404-881-2100, FoxTheatre.org*

Insider Tip: Tours are frequently cancelled due to performances and production schedules, so call ahead to verify tour dates!

HIGH MUSEUM OF ART - The High Museum of Art was founded in 1905 and gained a permanent home in the High family residence when it was donated in 1926. In 1983 the museum moved to its present location and became the Southeast's leading art museum. The High welcomes almost 500,000 visitors annually and houses a collection of over 11,000 works. Photography and folk art exhibits are housed in the Georgia Pacific Center downtown. *1280 Peachtree Street, 404-577-6940, High.org*

Insider Tip: The museum's growth has continued and necessitated the need for new space. Be sure to check the progress of new additions scheduled to open soon when you visit!

JIMMY CARTER LIBRARY & MUSEUM – Part of the Presidential Library System, the Jimmy Carter Library & Museum features photographs and historic memorabilia from the Carter presidency (1976 to 1981) and also from the personal life of Jimmy Carter. You'll find an exact replica of the Oval Office and some of the gifts received by the Carters. *441 Freedom Parkway, 404-865-7100, JimmyCarterLibrary.org*

MARGARET MITCHELL HOUSE & MUSEUM – Covering two blocks and including covered porches and a sunken garden, this 100-year-old house—listed on the National Register of Historic Places—is where Margaret Mitchell wrote her Pulitzer Prize-winning novel, *Gone with the Wind*. She lived in the house between 1925 and 1932 after it was turned into a 10–unit apartment complex (she lived in apartment #1). Although it was the victim of arson in 1994 and 1996 (just 40 days before the Summer Olympic Games), the house has since been renovated and restored. *999 Peachtree Street, 404-260-0821, GWTW.org*

Insider Tip: Don't miss the *Gone with the Wind* Movie Museum while you're there!

MARTIN LUTHER KING, JR. HISTORIC SITE – Martin Luther King, Jr. was born in 1929 on the second floor of 501 Auburn Avenue. Today you can still visit the Martin Luther King, Jr. Historic Site in Sweet Auburn, the prosperous black community that he called home. Even though he was assassinated in 1968, his vision lives on with the help of his wife Coretta Scott King, who is also a strong advocate for gay rights. *The King Center, 449 Auburn Avenue, 404-331-6922, TheKingCenter.org*

Insider Tip: Down the street you'll also find Ebenezer Baptist Church, where Martin Luther King, Jr. and his father, Martin Luther King, were pastors.

THE NAMES PROJECT FOUNDATION, INC – The Names Project Foundation heads-up the AIDS Memorial Quilt. Established in 1987, more than 91,000 names and 45,000 panels now comprise the quilt that is housed at the Foundation's office. Make a panel and donate it for free, or volunteer for administration and sewing activities. It's worth a visit to see the quilt and the breathtaking history that's memorialized within it. Tours and information are always available by calling the foundation. *101 Krog Street, 404-688-5500, AIDSQuilt.org*

SIX FLAGS OVER GEORGIA – Six Flags Over Georgia is a theme park with roller coasters, musical shows, and thrilling rides. It's a great place to go for a day of fun with a group of friends. *275 Riverside Parkway, Austell, 770-948-9290 SixFlags.com/Parks/OverGeorgia*

Insider Tip: In June Six Flags holds Pearl Day, which is their version of Disney's Gay Days.

Did You Know?

The longest escalator in the Southeast (over 192 feet) is located at MARTA's Peachtree Center Station.

SIX FLAGS WHITE WATER – If you like to get wet, you'll love Six Flag's sister park, White Water. Open every summer, White Water features a multitude of exciting water slides and attractions Including the Cliffhanger—one of the tallest freefalls in the world. *250 Cobb Parkway North, Marietta, 770-948-9290, SixFlags.com/Parks/WhiteWater*

STONE MOUNTAIN PARK – Stone Mountain is the world's largest mass of exposed granite, located on 3,200 gorgeous acres 16 miles east of downtown Atlanta. The centerpiece of the Park—and one of the true marvels of Western engineering—is found on the mountain's North side, where you'll see the world's largest relief carving, which depicts three heroes of the American Confederacy. *Highway 78 East, Stone Mountain, 770-498-5690, StoneMountainPark.com*

Insider Tip: Check out Stone Mountain's world-famous laser show, which runs from March until April. Call or visit their Web site for more information.

WALKING TOURS OF HISTORIC ATLANTA – Conducted by the Atlanta Preservation Center, Walking Tours of Historic Atlanta showcases the history of Atlanta from the Civil War to the Civil Rights Movement. Tours run from March to November and include the Fox Theatre, Historic Downtown, Sweet Auburn, the Martin Luther King, Jr. Historic District, Inman Park, Miss Daisy's Druid Hills, Grant Park, and Ansley Park. *Atlanta Preservation Center, 404-688-3350, PreserveAtlanta.com*

Insider Tip: Call ahead for times and start locations.

THE WORLD OF COCA-COLA – Learn all about the world's most popular soft drink at the World of Coca-Cola. Located in a three-story pavilion adjacent to Underground Atlanta, the museum showcases the rich history of Coke, which was created in Atlanta over 100 years ago. *55 Martin Luther King, Jr. Drive, 404-676-5151, WOCCAtlanta.com*

Insider Tip: Coca-Cola was first served in a small drugstore near Underground Atlanta, today it is available in more than 200 countries. At the end of the tour, you'll be able to sample as much Coke as you want from all of them!

ZOO ATLANTA – Located in historic Grant Park, Zoo Atlanta houses a variety of animals from all over the world. Recent exhibits have included the Giant Pandas of Chengdu, Orangutans of Ketambe, the Sumatran Tiger Forest, the World of Reptiles, Red Pandas, Monkeys of Makokou, and Asian Otters. *Grant Park, 800 Cherokee Avenue, 404-624-5600, ZooAtlanta.org*

Insider Tip: We recommend not using Internet mapping sites to find the Zoo. The best way is to call 888-945-5432 for directions.

Did You Know?

Atlanta has the largest unsupported escalator in the Southeast (8 stories tall) at CNN Center.

In This Chapter
Fitness Center • Gyms • Health Clubs • Yoga Studios

sweat

If you need to let off a little steam (or you simply want to relax in a steam room), check out any of the gyms and health clubs below. All are gay-friendly and offer specially priced daily, weekly, and even monthly workout plans. Call to find out more info.

BIKRAM YOGA – Feel like sweating? Bikram Yoga on Cheshire Bridge Road is designed to work the body from the inside with the help of a heated room (106 degrees). This type of yoga is said to benefit the organs, glands, and nervous system. *2000 Cheshire Bridge Road, 404-636-7535, bikramyogaatlanta.com*

Insider Tip: First-time students are asked to arrive 20 minutes before class time and to dress light.

COLONY SQUARE ATHLETIC CLUB – Convenient to MARTA, the Colony Square Athletic Club is a full-service fitness center offering extensive group classes and individual training along with traditional weight and aerobic machines. *1197 Peachtree Street, 404-745-9309, ColonyAthletic.com*

FITNESS FACTORY – Located in the same shopping center as Red Chair Video Lounge (see listing under *Play*),

Fitness Factory boasts a 12,000 square-foot facility along with Liquid Assets, a smoothie bar serving up delicious concoctions. Fitness Factory offers a choice of 49 fitness classes every week, including yoga, pilates, core ball, abs, meditation, boot camp, and spinning. *500 Amsterdam Avenue, Suite N, 404-815-7900, FFATL.com*

L.A. FITNESS @ Ansley Mall – L.A. Fitness offers tons of classes (including yoga several times a day), easy parking, and lots of eateries nearby for an after-workout meal or protein smoothie. *1544 Piedmont Avenue (Monroe Drive), 404-249-6463, LA Fitness.com*

Insider Tip: Dress to impress—this location is definitely NOT on cruise control!

L.A. FITNESS MIDTOWN @ Technology Square – This L.A. Fitness location near the Georgia Tech campus offers lots of free weights and new machines. *75 5th Street (Spring Street), 404-249-6404, LAFitness.com*

Insider Tip: A bit more laid back than the Ansley Mall location, you'll find a mixed crowd of college students from Georgia Tech and Georgia State, metrosexuals, and gym bunnies.

URBAN BODY FITNESS – Enjoy complimentary coffee and towel service at this 15,000 square-foot locally owned fitness facility. Known for its friendly staff, urban loft workout environment, and a separate building just for classes, this gym inspired a cult-like following. *742 Ponce De Leon Place, 404-885-1499, UrbanBodyFitness.com*

Did You Know?

Atlanta has the largest cable-supported domed stadium in North America—the Georgia Dome. *One Georgia Dome Drive, 404-223-4636, GADome.com.*

In This Chapter

Salons • Spas • Tanning

relax

If after a little too much shopping, playing, and working out your face and body need a little exfoliation or deep-tissue massage, head over to one of these spas or salons. All are gay-friendly and offer specialty services just for us boys (laser hair removal, anyone?). So take a day off and repeat to yourself: "It's all about me!"

COBALT – This full-service salon and spa offers skincare, laser hair removal, body treatments, and nail services. *1959 Piedmont Road, 404-249-1661, CobaltSalon.org*

ERIC LOW SALON – Called "shabby chic" by *Allure* magazine, Eric Low Salon offers hair styling, massage, facials, makeovers, waxing, and nail services. Described as "real beauty from real people," it's a perfect choice if you're looking for a comfortable environment without all the drama you might find at other salons. *814 Juniper Street, 404-607-8181, EricLowSalonSpa.com*

FRESCHE HAIR STUDIO – Located in an early 1900s Grant Park movie theater, Fresche Hair Salon has preserved the original theater lobby floor, exposed brick walls and a loft that once housed the theater's projector. Out of all the salons in Atlanta, Fresche was selected to host the makeover on the Discovery/Health Channel's National Body Challenge. *452-A Cherokee Avenue, 404-222-0244, Fresche.net*

HELMET – Helmet is a full-service salon for every beauty need. If you're looking for color, waxing, massages, or manicures, you'll find them all here. Stop by the newly renovated shop and check out the selection of products in the boutique. In *Southern Voice's* Best of Gay Atlanta, Helmet was voted "Best Salon" in 2003 and 2004. They definitely love their gay clientele! *970 Piedmont Avenue, 404-815-1629*

JAMES MADISON SALON – This high-tech salon offers services from cuts to colors and everything in-between. Stylists are trained by highly-respected companies like Bumble & Bumble and Vidal Sassoon. *929 Peachtree Street (The Metropolis), 404-266-8617, JamesMadisonSalon.com*

JOQ DAY SPA – This upscale men-only spa offers massage, facials, manicures and pedicures, laser hair removal, Botox, and more. JOQ features Guy Gear as well as their own JOQ brand line of products, which was featured on E!'s *Celebrity Beauty Secrets*. JOQ knows that ATLANTAboys will be more comfortable with an all-male clientele. In other words: No girls allowed! *1545 Peachtree Street, Suite 210 (Lobby Level), 404-892-7771, JOQ.com*

KEY LIME PIE – This serene full-service salon and wellness spa in Virginia-Highlands offers a retreat from life's everyday stresses. This cozy hideaway offers facials, hair removal, manicures, pedicures, and wet treatments such as their Aquatherapy Body Polish. *806 North Highland Avenue, 404-873-6512, KeyLimePie.net*

RICHIE ARPINO SALON – This cozy salon and spa was voted "Best Haircut in Atlanta" by *Allure* magazine. Along with Buckhead Betties and ATLANTAboys, the salon has

relax

also catered to the likes of Julia Roberts, Brooke Shields, Darryl Hannah, Nikki Taylor, Kevin Costner, Melissa Etheridge and Jennifer Tilly. *3201 Paces Ferry Place, 404-231-5092, ArpinoSalon.com*

SOLARIUM – Need a tan and need it now? Head over to Solarium, where you'll find an array of sunshine options, including Ultra Class Magic, Sunsport Platinum HP and VHR-Onyx. There are also Mystic Tan spray booths for those of you who are UV-conscious. The Solarium was also named one of the top tanning salons in the U.S. three years in a row by *Looking Fit Magazine*. *939 Peachtree Street, 404-815-4899, SolarDimensions.com*

VAN MICHAEL – This respected full-service Aveda-Lifestyle salon caters to Atlanta's desperate housewives as well as lots of ATLANTAboys. Since 1992, this family-owned salon in two locations (Buckhead and Virginia-Highlands) has cut the hair of local and national celebrities, who head inside for a little mid-day energy infusion. *39 West Paces Ferry Road, 404-237-4664 and 778 North Highland Avenue, 404-874-6604, VanMichael.com*

Insider Tip: Feeling a little wallet-conscious? Head next door to New Talents Salon, where a Van Michael trainee will cut your hair for half the price. *39 West Paces Fevry Road, 404-261-3965.*

Did You Know?

Atlanta has the tallest hotel in North America—the Westin Peachtree Plaza—at 73 stories (723 feet tall). *210 Peachtree Street, 404-659-1400, Westin.com/Peachtree.*

In This Chapter

Rugby • Cycling • Football • Tennis • Track • Soccer • Softball • Swimming / Diving • Volleyball

sports

If thinking about sports makes you want to grab a bat and ball (or just balls), you'll find plenty of other ATLANTAboys who share the same interest as you. Many teams and associations in Atlanta promote camaraderie through sports and team interaction, so why not join in the fun? Whether you play for this team or that team, just remember: we all play for the same team!

ATLANTA BUCKS RUGBY FOOTBALL CLUB – Rugby may not be your usual gay sport, but the Atlanta Bucks Rugby Football Club was founded in 2003 for the gay community to provide a fraternal environment free from discrimination to build a competitive team. *AtlantaBucksRugby.org*

ACTION CYCLING ATLANTA – Action Cycling Atlanta is a group of cyclists from diverse backgrounds—gay and straight—who have a common interest in physical fitness and philanthropy. So far they have raised over $70,000 for AIDS vaccine research. The organization donates 100% of money raised to its beneficiaries. *678-592-2258, ActionCycling.org*

ATLANTA RAINBOW TROUT – Atlanta Rainbow Trout is a gay-friendly aquatics club for those who love swimming, triathlon, water polo, and generally getting wet. Over the past eight years they have become one of the most respected sports organizations in Atlanta. *404-286-6131, AtlantaRainbowTrout.com*

ATLANTA TEAM TENNIS ASSOCIATION - The local chapter of the Gay and Lesbian Tennis Alliance is the Atlanta Team Tennis Association. With over 340 members, it's the largest organization of its kind. The ATTA plays a variety of matches—from open play social round robin to league team play. There are also player development clinics available. *ATTA.org*

ATLANTA THUNDER FOOTBALL – Formed in 2002, Atlanta Thunder Football is a diverse flag-football team has been playing informally for seven years. The team is a nonprofit organization dedicated to the promotion of sport and fellowship in Atlanta. They practice and play throughout the year in preparation for the National Gay Flag-Football Tournament which is held each year in Atlanta. *404-307-4802, AtlantaThunderFootball.com*

FRONTRUNNERS – Frontrunners provides encouragement and support to lesbians and gay men who enjoy running or walking. Their mission is to promote healthy living and socializing through physical fitness. The group hosts weekly run-walks and also sponsors fundraisers for local charities. *770-621-5007, FrontRunnersAtlanta.org*

HOTLANTA SOCCER ASSOCIATION – The Hotlanta Soccer Association was formed to provide Atlantans with a gay-friendly alternative to other adult soccer leagues. They compete locally in Atlanta soccer leagues as well as in tournaments throughout the world. Organized by the International Gay and Lesbian Football Association, tournaments are held several times throughout the year in cities ranging from Ft. Lauderdale to Berlin with players of all skill levels. *HotlantaSoccer.com*

sports

HOTLANTA SOFTBALL – Since 1981, Hotlanta Softball has played a spring and fall season and is a member of the National Association of Gay Amateur Athletic Alliance. They offer two divisions of play: a women's division for women only and an open division composed mainly of men, but also including a few female players. *HotlantaSoftball.org*

HOTLANTA VOLLEYBALL ASSOCIATION – Hotlanta Volleyball Association is a nonprofit organization founded for gay volleyball lovers. The group is a member of the North American Gay Volleyball Association and sponsors many activities throughout the year. They also make donations of time and money to local Atlanta charities. *HotlantaVolleyball.org*

Did You Know?

Atlanta is home to the Peachtree Road Race, the largest 10K race in the world with 55,000 runners annually.

In This Chapter

Associations • Charities • Foundations • Fundraising • Nonprofits • Volunteer

give

As we've all learned from Kabbalah, it's more important to give than receive. Or was it the more you give, the more you receive? In any case, choosing to help out one of the local charitable organizations is bound to make you feel all warm and fuzzy inside.

THE ARMORETTES – The Armorettes are a raunchy, raucous bunch of um...*girls*. This group of "ladies" doesn't perform the type of drag that you're used to—instead, these camp drag performers stage some of the funniest numbers you'll ever see. Since their inception in 1980, they've strutted through over 50,000 routines, entertained hundreds of thousands of people, donned countless pairs of bad shoes and high-hair wigs, and raised over $1.4 million for worthy causes. Be sure to catch their shows Sunday nights at Burkhart's (see listing under *Play*)! *Armorettes.com*

AID ATLANTA – AID Atlanta is an AIDS services organization that serves individuals living with AIDS through education. They work to reduce at-risk behavior to help stop the spread of HIV and empower Georgians to live independent and productive lives. AID Atlanta's direct services and outreach programs are critical in teaching the community about AIDS. *1438 West Peachtree Street, Suite 100, 404-870-7700, AidAtlanta.org*

AIDS SURVIVIAL PROJECT – AIDS Survival Project is a diverse group of people who work to promote self-empowerment and enhanced quality of life for HIV-affected people through education, advocacy, peer support, and treatment. *159 Ralph McGill Boulevard, Suite 500, 404-874-7926, AIDSSurvivalProject.org*

ATLANTA EXECUTIVE NETWORK (AEN) – Atlanta Executive Network is one of the largest networking organizations in the country. Founded in 1992, the group has four goals: to promote business and social contacts through networking; to advocate equality for the lesbian, gay, bisexual and transgender community; to promote diversity in the business community; and to foster leadership in business, government and the arts. You can post your resume on the group's Web site and attend monthly luncheons for networking in an intimate environment. *1379 Tullie Road, Suite 101, 404-321-0079, AEN.org*

ATLANTA PRIDE COMMITTEE – The Atlanta Pride Committee produces the annual Pride Festival and Parade. The Festival is held each year on the last weekend in June to commemorate the Stonewall Riots, which launched the modern GLBT rights movement. The festival typically attracts over 300,000 people and hosts a variety of performers, artists, community and food booths, and with special guest speakers. There is also a Pride Parade through Midtown on the last day of the festival. *57 Executive Park South, Suite 380, 404-929-0071, AtlantaPride.org*

CHRIS RAINBOW HOME – The Rainbow Home was founded as a division of CHRIS Homes to provide a positive, safe, and supportive home for homeless and runaway gay, lesbian, bisexual, transgender, and questioning youth. The home also provides life-skills training by partnering with community resources, counseling, medical, and legal services. CHRIS is one of only a handful of homes like it in the U.S., and the only program of its kind in the Southeast. *404-457-1721, CHRISKids.org*

GEORGIA EQUALITY – Georgia's gay, lesbian, bisexual, and transgender citizens and their friends have an advocate in an organization called Georgia Equality. Their mission is to secure political and economic equality for the GLBT communities of Georgia through education, grassroots organizing and political advocacy. They aim to form policies and alliances with state and local political officials to reach their goals. *1379 Tullie Road, 404-327-9898, GeorgiaEquality.org*

THE NAMES PROJECT FOUNDATION, INC.
(See listing under *Visit*)

P.A.L.S. (PETS ARE LOVING SUPPORT) – P.A.L.S. provides support and care for the pets of Atlanta-area residents who are living with critical illnesses and disabilities. The organization was founded when two businesswomen met a man living with AIDS who was sharing his only meal each day with his cat. They were so moved by his situation that they began collecting pet food. The first Thursday of each month, P.A.L.S. sponsors Bingo Night, hosted by *Out* magazine's "Hottest Drag Queen," Bubba D. Licious. *1058-C Northside Drive, 404-876-PALS, PALSAtlanta.org*

PFLAG ATLANTA – PFLAG offers education and support to the families and friends of gay, lesbian, bisexual, and transgender people. There are over 250,000 PFLAG members nationwide in more than 500 affiliates. Through this network, PFLAG dispels myths and misinformation by working with educators, community and religious groups, the media, and the general public. *850 Dogwood Road, Suite 400, Box 480, Lawrenceville, 770-662-6475, PFLAGATL.org*

PROJECT OPEN HAND – This organization operates like an assembly line. Volunteers work around the clock to prepare nutritional meals and to deliver them to people living with symptomatic HIV and AIDS, homebound seniors, and individuals with other critical illnesses or disabilities. In 1988, a small crew began cooking meals for 14 people. Project Open Hand has since grown to 50 employees who produce 3,000 meals daily. *176 Ottley Drive, 404-872-8089, ProjectOpenHand.org*

YOUTH PRIDE – YouthPride is the only organization in metro Atlanta serving GLBT teenagers (13 to 17) and young adults (18 to 24). The group's goal is to provide a safe-haven for all youth, regardless of gender identity and expression, HIV infection, parental custody, educational enrollment, handicap, race and ethnicity, or income. They also participate in and support programs, activities, and events with other GLBT organizations in the Atlanta community. *302 East Howard Avenue, 404-378-6620, YouthPride.org*

Did You Know?

The AIDS Memorial Quilt is housed and based in Atlanta at the Names Project Foundation? The quilt began in 1987 with a single name on a 3 x 6 panel. Today it includes more than 91,000 names on more than 45,000 panels, standing as the largest piece of community art in the world and serving as a living memorial to those lost to AIDS. Although sections of the quilt are on display throughout the world, you can call the Names Project Foundation to set up a tour of the foundation for individuals or groups. *101 Krog Street, 404-688-5500, AIDSQuilt.org*

In This Chapter

Blogs • Magazines • Newspapers • Web Sites

read

- **ABOUT.COM** – Web Site (Free) – *Atlanta.About.com*

- **ACCESSATLANTA** – Newspaper (Free) – *72 Marietta Street, 404-526-5151, AccessAtlanta.com*

- **ARJAN WRITES** – Blog (Free) – *ArjanWrites.com*

- **ATLANTA.NET** – Web Site (Free) – *Atlanta Convention & Visitors Bureau, 233 Peachtree Street, Suite 100, 404-521-6600, Atlanta.net*

- **ATLANTA ENTERTAINMENT ONLINE** – Web Site (Free) – *AtlantaEntertainment.com*

- **ATLSINGLEMAN!** – Blog (Free) - *ATLSingleMan.com*

- **ATLANTA MAGAZINE** – Magazine (Purchase) – *260 Peachtree Street, Suite 300, 404-527-5500, AtlantaMagazine.com*

- **ATLANTABOY** – Blog (Free) - *925-B Peachtree Street, 404-745-8636, ATLANTAboy.com*

- **ATLANTA INTOWNCONSTITUTION** – Newspaper (Free) - *1280 West Peachtree Street Suite 220, 404-586-0002, AtlantaNewsGroup.com*

- **ATLANTA JOURNAL-CONSTITUTION** – Newspaper (Purchase) - *72 Marietta Street, 404-526-5151, AJC.com*

- **CITYSEARCH** – Web Site (Free)–*Atlanta.Citysearch.com*

- **CREATIVE LOAFING** – Newspaper (Free) - *750 Willoughby Way, 404-688-5623, Atlanta.CreativeLoafing.com*

- **DAVID ATLANTA** – Magazine (Free) - *1075 Zonolite Road, Suite 1-D, 404-876-1819, DavidAtlanta.com*

- **JEZEBEL** – Magazine (Purchase) - *3535 Piedmont Road, Building 14, Floor 12, 404-870-0123, JezebelMagazine.com*

- **MIDTOWN MAGAZINE** – Magazine (Free)–*1076 Canton Street, Roswell, 770-992-7808, NWPublications.com*

- **PAPER CITY** – Newspaper (Free)–*1776 Peachtree Road, Suite 200-S, 404-591-3145, PaperCityMag.com*

- **THE PIEDMONT REVIEW** – Newspaper (Free)–*P.O. Box 12047, 404-560-3677, PiedmontReview.com*

- **SOUTHERN VOICE** – Newspaper (Free) - *1075 Zonolite Road, Suite 1-D, 404-876-1819, SoVo.com*

- **THE SUNDAY PAPER** – Newspape (Free)–*763 Trabert Avenue, Suite D, 404-351-5797, SundayPaper.com*

Did You Know?

Atlanta houses the largest toll-free telephone dialing area in the world with over 7,000 miles of toll-free calling.

It also has the largest suburban office park in the United States—Perimeter Center—with 3.5 million square feet of office and retail space on 400 acres.

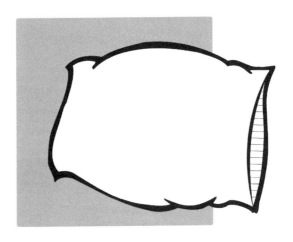

In This Chapter

Inexpensive Motels • Mid-Priced Lodging • Luxury Hotels • Bed & Breakfasts • Youth Hostels

stay

Inexpensive Motels

- Cheshire Motor Inn – *1865 Cheshire Bridge Road, 404-872-9628*
- The Highland Inn – *644 North Highland Avenue, 404-874-5756*
- Lenox Inn – *3387 Lenox Road, 404-261-5500*
- Midtown Inn – *1470 Spring Street, 404-872-5821*
- Paschal Motor Hotel – *830 Martin Luther King, Jr. Drive, 404-577-3150*
- Residence Inn – *1365 Peachtree Street, 404-872-8885, ResidenceInn.com*
- Sierra Suites – *3967 Peachtree Street, 404-873-5731, SierraSuites.com*
- Travelodge Atlanta Downtown – *311 Courtland Street, 404-659-4545, AtlantaTravelodge.com*

Mid-Priced Lodging

- Atlanta Marriott Suites – *35 14th Street, 404-876-8888, Marriott.com*
- Best Western Inn at the Peachtrees – *330 West Peachtree Street, 404-577-6970, BestWestern.com*
- Courtyard by Marriott – *1132 Techwood Drive, 404-607-1112, Marriott.com*
- Embassy Suites Hotel – *3285 Peachtree Road, 404-261-7733, EmbassySuites.com*

- Fairfield Inn – *1470 Spring Street, 404-872-5821, Marriott.com*
- Georgia Tech Hotel & Conference Center – *800 Spring Street, 404-347-9440, GaTechHotel.com*
- Granada Suites Hotel – *1302 West Peachtree Street, 404-876-6100*
- Homewood Suites – *3566 Piedmont Road, 404-365-0001, Homewood-Suites.com*
- Hotel Indigo – *683 Peachtree Street, 404-874-9200, HotelIndigo.com*
- The Omni Hotel at CNN Center – *100 CNN Center, 404-659-0000, OmniHotels.com*
- Renaissance Hotel – *590 West Peachtree Street, 404-881-6000, Marriott.com*
- Sheraton Midtown Atlanta Hotel at Colony Square – *188 14th Street, 404-892-6000, Sheraton.com*
- The Suite Hotel at Underground – *54 Peachtree Street, 404-223-5555, SuiteHotel.com*
- Westin Buckhead – *3391 Peachtree Road, 404-365-0065, Westin.com*

Luxury Hotels

- Four Seasons Hotel – *75 14th Street, 404-881-9898, FourSeasons.com*
- Georgian Terrace Hotel – *659 Peachtree Street, 404-897-1991, The GeorgianTerrace.com*
- Grand Hyatt Atlanta – *3300 Peachtree Road, 404-365-8100, Hyatt.com*
- InterContinental Atlanta Hotel – *3315 Peachtree Road, 404-946-9000 InterContinental.com*
- Ritz Carlton – *181 Peachtree Street, 404-659-0400; 3434 Peachtree Road, 404-237-2700, RitzCarlton.com*

stay

- Westin Buckhead – *3391 Peachtree Road, 404-365-0065, Westin.com*
- Westin Peachtree Plaza – *210 Peachtree Street, 404-659-1400, Westin.com*

Bed & Breakfasts

- Ansley Inn – *253 15th Street, 404-870-0368, AnsleyInn.com*
- Gaslight Inn – *1001 St Charles Avenue, 404-875-1001, GaslightInn.com*
- Hello Bed & Breakfast – *1865 Windemere Drive, 404-892-8111, Members.AOL.com/HelloBnB*
- Inman Park Bed & Breakfast – *100 Waverly Way, 404-688-9498, InmanParkBandB.com*
- King Keith House – *889 Edgewood Avenue, 404-688-7330, KingKeith.com*
- Shellmont Inn – *821 Piedmont Avenue, 404-872-9290, Shellmont.com*
- Sugar Magnolia Bed & Breakfast – *804 Edgewood Avenue, 404-222-0226, SugarMagnoliuBB.com*
- Stonehurst Bed & Breakfast – *923 Piedmont Avenue, 404-881-5324, StonehurstBandB.com*
- Virginia Highland Bed & Breakfast – *630 Orme Circle, 404-892-2735, VirginiaHighlandBB.com*

Youth Hostels

- Atlanta Youth Hostel – *229 Ponce de Leon Avenue, 404-875-2882, Hostel-Atlanta.com*
- Hello Bed & Breakfast – *1865 Windemere Drive, 404-892-8111, Members.AOL.com/Hellobnb*

In This Chapter

January • February • March • April • May • June • July • August • September • October • November • December

annual events

JANUARY

- Dr. Martin Luther King Jr. Celebration – *Atlanta, 404-524-1956*
- Peach Bowl – *Georgia Dome, 404-223-9200, PeachBowl.com*
- Resolution Run 2K/5K/10K – *Technology Park, Norcross, 770-231-9064*
- Stone Mountain 5 Mile & 10 Mile – *Stone Mountain Park, 404-231-9064*

FEBRUARY

- Atlanta Film Festival – *Atlanta, 404-352-4225, ImageFV.org*
- Black History Month Celebration – *404-330-6630*
- Ringling Bros. Barnum & Bailey Circus – *Philips Arena, 404-249-6400, Ringling.com*
- Southeastern Flower Show – *404-888-5638, FlowerShow.org*

ATLANTAboy: An Insider's Guide to Gay Atlanta

Did You Know?

Atlanta has the oldest continually operated ballet company in the nation—The Atlanta Ballet—since 1929.

MARCH

- Atlanta International Car Show – *Georgia World Congress Center – 404-223-4636, 800-258-8912*
- Conyers Cherry Blossom Festival – *Conyers, 770-918-2169, ConyersCherryBlossom.com*
- St. Patrick's Day Parade – Downtown & Buckhead – *404-330-6630*

APRIL

- Atlanta Dogwood Festival – *Piedmont Park, 404-329-0501, Dogwood.org*
- Easter Sunrise Service – *Stone Mountain Park, 770-498-5600*
- Georgia Renaissance Festival – *Fairburn, 770-964-8575, GARenFest.com*
- Inman Park Festival & Tour of Homes – *Inman Park, 770-242-4895, InmanPark.org*
- Midtown Tour of Homes – Midtown, *404-607-7230, MidtownTourOfHomes.com*
- March of Dimes WalkAmerica – *Centennial Olympic Park, Atlanta, 404-350-9800, MarchOfDimes.com*

annual events

MAY

- Atlanta Jazz Festival – *Grant Park & Underground Atlanta, 404-817-6815, AtlantaFestivals.com*
- Georgia Special Olympics – *Emory University, 404-521-6600, SpecialOlympicsGA.org*
- KingFest International – *Martin Luther King, Jr. Center for Nonviolent Social Change, 404-893-9882*

JUNE

- Pride – *Piedmont Park, 404-330-6630, AtlantaPride.org*
- Atlanta Symphony Orchestra Summer Concert Series – *Chastain Park Amphitheater, 404-733-5000, AtlantaSymphony.org*
- Georgia Shakespeare Festival – *Oglethorpe University, 404-264-0020, GAShakespeare.org*
- Virginia Highland SummerFest – *404-222-9244, VaHi.org*
- Pearl Day Six Flags, *770-948-9290, SixFlags.com/Parks/OverGeorgia*
- Music Midtown Festival – Midtown, *770-MIDTOWN, MusicMidtown.com*

JULY

- Peachtree Road Race 10K, *Lenox Mall to Piedmont Park, 404-231-9065*
- Salute 2 America Parade – *Downtown, 404-897-7000*
- Star Spangled Night – *Lenox Square, 404-233-6767*
- Summer Film Series – *Fox Theatre, 404-817-8700, FoxTheatre.org*

AUGUST

- Black Gay Pride – *Atlanta, InTheLifeATL.com*

SEPTEMBER

- Atlanta Greek Festival – *Greek Orthodox Cathedral of the Annunciation – 404-633-5870, ATLGOC.org/Festival.htm*
- Candler Park/Lake Claire Music & Arts Festival – *Candler Park, 404-377-1803, CandlerPark.org/Festival*
- Candler Park Tour of Funky Homes – *Candler Park, 404-377-1803, CandlerPark.org/HomeTours*
- Grant Park Tour of Homes – *Grant Park, 404-330-6630, GrantPark.org*
- Labor Day Weekend Festival – *Underground Atlanta, 404-521-6600, Underground-Atlanta.com*
- Taste of Atlanta – *Peachtree & 10th Street, 404-521-6600, TasteOfAtlanta.org*

OCTOBER

- AIDS Walk – Midtown, *404-876-WALK, Walk.AIDAtlanta.org*
- Georgia Shakespeare Festival – *Oglethorpe University – 404-264-0020, GAShakespeare.org*

NOVEMBER

- Atlanta International Film Festival – *Phipps Plaza, 404-816-4262, AtlantaFilmFestival.com*

DECEMBER

- Atlanta Symphony Orchestra Holiday Concerts – *Symphony Hall, 404-733-4900, AtlantaSymphony.org*

annual events

- Peach Drop – *Underground Atlanta, 404-523-2311, Underground-Atlanta.com*
- First Night Atlanta – *Midtown, 404-881-0400, FirstNightAtlanta.com*
- The Nutcracker, *Fox Theatre, 404-817-8700, FoxTheatre.org*
- Peach Bowl Parade – *Downtown, 404-330-6630, PeachBowl.com*

Did You Know?

Stone Mountain Park has the world's largest bas-relief sculpture and the world's largest exposed mass of granite. *Highway 78 East, Stone Mountain, 770-498-5690, StoneMountainPark.com.*

In This Chapter

Baptists • Catholic • Christian • Episcopal • Jewish • Lutheran • Methodist • Metropolitan Community Church • Presbyterian • Unitarian Universalist • Unity

worship

Baptist

- **OAKHURST BAPTIST CHURCH** - 222 East Lake Drive, 404-378-3677, OakhurstBaptist.org

Catholic

- **CATHOLIC SHINE OF THE IMMACULATE CONCEPTION** - 48 Martin Luther King, Jr. Drive, 404-521-1866, CatholicShrineAtlanta.org
- **ST. MICHAEL THE DEFENDER CATHOLIC CHURCH** - 1071 Delaware Avenue, 404-627-7212, StMichaelAtlanta.org

Christian

- **NEW COVENANT CHURCH OF ATLANTA** - 743 Virginia Avenue, 404-881-6336, SavedAndGay.com
- **VIRGINIA HIGHLAND CHURCH** - 743 Virginia Avenue, 404-873-1355, VHChurch.net

Episcopal

- **ALL SAINTS EPISCOPAL CHURCH** - 634 West Peachtree Street, 404-881-0835, AllSaintsAtlanta.org
- **THE CATHEDRAL OF ST. PHILIP** - 2744 Peachtree Road, 404-365-1000, StPhilipCathedral.org

- **ST. BARTHOLOMEW'S EPISCOPAL CHURCH** - *1790 LaVista Road, 404-634-3336, StBartsAtlanta.org*
- **ST. LUKE'S EPISCOPAL CHURCH** - *435 Peachtree Street, 404-873-7600, StLukesAtlanta.org*

Jewish

- **CONGREGATION BET HAVERIM** - *Central Congregation Church, 2676 Clairmont Road, 404-315-6446*

Lutheran

- **ST. JOHN'S LUTHERAN CHURCH** - *1410 Ponce de Leon Avenue, 404-378-4243, StJohnsAtlanta.org*

Methodist

- **ST. MARK UNITED METHODIST CHURCH** - *781 Peachtree Street, 404-873-2636, StMarkUMC.org*

Metropolitan Community Church

- **CHRIST COVENANT MCC** - *109 Hibernia Avenue, 404-373-2933, ChristCovenantMCC.org*
- **FIRST METROPOLITAN COMMUNITY CHURCH** - *1379 Tully Road, 404-325-4143, FirstMCC.com*

Presbyterian

- **DRUID HILLS PRESBYTERIAN CHURCH** - *1026 Ponce de Leon Avenue, 404-875-7591, DHPC.org*
- **ORMEWOOD PARK PRESBYTERIAN CHURCH** - *1071 Delaware Avenue, 404-627-2216, OrmewoodParkPres.org*

Unitarian Universalist

- **FIRST EXISTENTIALIST CONGREGATION OF ATLANTA** - *470 Candler Park Drive, 404-378-5570, First Existentialist.org*

Unity

- **UNITY FELLOWSHIP CHURCH** - *2001 Martin Luther King, Jr. Drive, 404-752-5030, UnityFellowshipChurchAtl.org*

Did You Know?

Atlanta is home to the largest museum in the world solely dedicated to a famous civil rights leader—the Martin Luther King, Jr. National Historic Site. *The King Center, 449 Auburn Avenue, 404-331-6922, TheKingCenter.org.*

In This Chapter

Resources

resources

Airlines

- AirTran – *800-AIRTRAN, AirTran.com*
- America West – *800-235-9292, AmericaWest.com*
- American Airlines – *800-433-7300, AA.com*
- Continental – *770-436-3300, Continental.com*
- Delta – *404-765-5000, Delta.com*
- Midwest Express – *800-452-2022, MidwestExpress.com*
- Northwest – *800-225-2525, NWA.com*
- United – *800-241-6522, United.com*
- USAirways – *800-428-4322, USAirways.com*

Alcohol & Drug Dependency

- Alcoholics Anonymous – *800-711-6375, AtlantaAAA.org*
- Alcohol Treatment Center – *800-711-1000*
- Alcohol & Drug Services – *404-851-8961*
- Drug HelpLine – *800-378-4435*
- Narcotics Anonymous – *800-711-6375, AtlantaAA.org*
- Substance Abuse – *800-234-0420*

Animals

- Animal Control – *404-794-0358*
- Animal Emergency Clinic – *404-252-7881*
- Humane Society – *404-875-5331, ATLHumane.org*

Automobiles

- American Automobile Association (AAA) – 404-843-4500, AAA.com
- Atlanta Impound Lot – 404-853-4330
- Georgia Department of Motor Vehicle Safety – 678-413-8400, DMVS.GA.gov
- Parking Violations – 404-658-6935
- State Department of Motor Vehicles – *Tag & Title Information*, 404-362-6500
- Traffic Court – 404-658-6940

City of Atlanta

- City of Atlanta Official Web Site – CI.Atlanta.GA.us
- Atlanta Assessor – 404-730-6400
- Atlanta City Council – 404-330-6030, Apps.AtlantaGA.gov/CityCoul
- Atlanta City Hall – 404-330-6000, AtlantaGA.gov
- Atlanta Mayor Shirley Franklin's Office – 404-330-6100, AtlantaGA.gov/Mayor

Consumer Complaints & Services

- Atlanta Bar Association – 404-521-0781, AtlantaBar.org
- Atlanta Chamber of Commerce – 404-880-9000, MACOC.com
- Better Business Bureau of Metropolitan Atlanta – 404-688-4910, Atlanta.BBB.org
- Consumer Products Safety Commission – 404-730-2870, CPSC.gov
- Federal Trade Commission – 877-FTC-HELP, FTC.gov
- State Attorney General Consumer Affairs Division – 404-656-3790, GANet.org/Ago

- State Insurance Commissioner – *404-656-2070, Inscomm.State.GA.us*
- State Consumer Affairs Office – *404-651-8600, 800-869-1123, GOCA.GA.gov*
- US Attorney General – *404-581-6000, GANet.org*
- US Public Interest Research Group (USPIRG) – *404-892-3403, PIRG.org*

County Office

- Fulton County Government – *404-730-4000, Co.Fulton.Ga.us*

Crime

- Crime in Progress – *911*
- Crime & Trauma Scene Cleanup Assistance – *888-979-2272*
- Atlanta Police Department – *404-330-6100, AtlantaPD.org*
- Atlanta PD Community Service Unit – *404-658-7032, AtlantaPD.org*
- Fulton County Police Department – *404-730-5700, FultonPolice.org*
- Georgia Office of Homeland Security – *GAHomelandSecurity.com*
- State Patrol Office – *404-657-9300*
- Victim-Witness Assistance Program – *404-865-8127*

Discrimination

- City of Atlanta Human Services Department – *404-817-6702, AtlantaGA.gov*
- Fulton County Human Services Department – *404-730-7944, Co.Fulton.GA.us*

- Georgia Commission on Equal Opportunity (Employment) – *404-656-1736, GCEO.State.GA.us*
- Georgia Commission on Equal Opportunity (Housing) – *404-656-7708, GCEO.State.GA.us*
- State Community Services Department – *404-679-4840*
- US Government Employment Discrimination Department – *800-669-4000*
- US Government Health & Human Services Discrimination Department – *800-368-1019*
- US Government Housing Discrimination Department – *800-669-9777*

Garbage & Sanitation

- Atlanta Public Works Department – *404-65WORKS, Co.Fulton.GA.us*
- Unincorporated Fulton County Garbage Pick Up – *404-730-7400*

Government & Elected Officials

- Atlanta Mayor Shirley Franklin's Office – *404-330-6100, AtlantaGA.gov/Mayor*
- Board of Elections (Fulton County) – *404-730-7072*
- Georgia Governor's Office – *404-656-1776, Gov.State.GA.us*
- Secretary of State – *404-656-2881, SOS.State.GA.us*

Entertainment

- Arts at Emory – *404-727-6187, Arts.Emory.edu*
- Arts Hotline – *404-853-3ART*
- Atlanta Coalition of Theatres – *404-873-1185, AtlantaTheatres.org*

- City of Atlanta Bureau of Cultural Affairs – *404-817-6815, BCAAtlanta.com*
- *Creative Loafing* Online Happenings Calendar – *Atlanta.CreativeLoafing.com*
- Dancer's Collective of Atlanta – *404-233-7600, DancersCollective.org*
- Fulton County Arts Council – *404-730-5780, FultonArts.org*
- 99Xtension Music Line – *404-364-0997, 99X.com*
- TicketMaster – *404-249-6400, Ticketmaster.com*

Health & Medical Care

- AIDS Hotline – *404-222-0800*
- AIDS Hotline – *CDC National, 800-342-AIDS, CDC.gov*
- AIDS Testing – *404-730-1401*
- American Cancer Society – *800-ACS-2345, Cancer.org*
- American Lung Association of Georgia – *770-434-5864, Lungs-USA.org*
- Board of Health – *404-730-1211*
- Diabetes Association of Atlanta – *404-527-7150, DiabetesAtlanta.org*
- Epilepsy Foundation – *404-527-7155, Epilepsy.GA.org*
- Poison Control Center (Metro Atlanta) – *404-616-9000, GPC.DHR.Georgia.gov*

Physician Referral Services

- Atlanta Medical Center Physician Referral – *404-265-3627, AtlantaMedCenter.com*
- Dentist Information Service – *800-917-6453, Dental-Referral.com*
- Millennium Alternative Healthcare – *770-390-0012*
- Promina Health System Physician Referral – *404-541-1111, Promina.org*

Legal Referral

- AAA Attorney Referral Service of Georgia – *404-252-8808*
- Atlanta Bar Association – *404-521-0777, AtlantaBar.org*
- Atlanta Volunteer Lawyers Foundation – *404-521-0790, AVLF.org*
- Legal Aid Services of Atlanta – *404-222-0843, LegalAid-GA.org*

Libraries

- Fulton County/City of Atlanta – *404-730-1700, AF.Public.Lib.GA.us*

Parks

- Fulton County Parks & Recreation Department – *404-730-6200, Co.Fulton.GA.us*
- Atlanta City Parks & Recreation Bureau – *404-817-6752, AtlantaGA.gov*

Parking Violations

- Atlanta Impound Lot – *404-853-4330*
- General Ticket Information – *404-658-6940*
- Parking Collections – *404-658-6886*
- Parking Violations – *404-658-6935*

Police

- Atlanta–*Emergency, 911; Business, 404-853-3434, AtlantaPD.org*
- Fulton County–*Emergency, 911; Business, 404-730-5700, Co.Fulton.GA.us/Police*

- Georgia State Patrol – *404-624-6077, DPS.Georgia.gov*
- U.S. Marshal's Service – *404-331-6833, USMarshalls.gov*

Post Office

- 800-111-1111, *USPS.gov*

Recycling

- City of Atlanta Recycling Hotline – *404-792-1212, AtlantaGA.gov*
- Fulton County Recycling Information – *770-925-3571, Co.Fulton.GA.us*

Shipping Services

- Airborne Express (AirEx) – *800-247-2676, Airborne.com*
- DHL Worldwide Express – *800-225-5345, DHL-USA.com*
- Federal Express (FedEx) – *800-463-3339, FedFx.com*
- Roadway Express – *404-361-0861, Roadway.com*
- United Parcel Service (UPS) – *800-742-5877, UPS.com*
- US Postal Service Express Mail – *800-222-1811, USPS.com*
- Delta Dash – 800-638-7333, *Delta.com/AirCargo*

Sports

- Atlanta Braves – *404-577-9100, AtlantaBraves.com*
- Atlanta Hawks – *404-827-3865, NBA.com/Hawks*
- Atlanta Falcons – *404-223-8000, NFL.com/Falcons*
- Atlanta Thrashers – *404-584-7825, AtlantaThrashers.com*
- The Masters – *706-667-6000, Masters.org*

- Clark Atlanta University Athletic Department – *404–880–8126, CAU.edu/Athletics*
- Emory University Athletic Department – *404–727–6547, Go.Emory.edu*
- Georgia State University Athletic Department – *404–651–2772, GeorgiaState.com/Sports*
- Georgia Tech Athletic Department – *404–894–5400, GATech.edu/Sports*
- Morehouse College Athletic Department – *404–215–2669, Morehouse.edu/Athletics*
- Morris Brown College Athletic Department – *404–220–3619, MorrisBrown.edu*
- Oglethorpe University Athletic Department – *404–364–8415, Oglethorpe.edu/Athletics*
- University of Georgia Athletic Department – *706–542–1621, Sports.UGA.edu*

State Government

- Georgia State Government - *State.GA.us*
- Georgia Secretary of State – *404–656–2881, SOS.State.GA.us*
- Governor's Office – *404–656–1776, GAGovernor.org*

Taxi Service

- AAA Yellow Cab of Metro Atlanta – *404–373–0034*
- Atlanta Yellow Cab Company – *404–521–0200*
- Buckhead Safety Cab – *404–233–1152, Buckhead.org/Transportation*
- Checker Cab Company – *404–351–1111,*

AtlantaCheckerCab.com
- Style Taxi – *404-522-8294, StyleTaxi.com*

Time

- *770-486-8834*

Tourism & Travel

- Atlanta Convention & Visitors Bureau – *404-521-6660, Atlanta.net*
- Georgia Tourist Information – *800-VISITGA, GoMM.com*
- State Parks & Historic Sites – 404-656-3530, *GAStateParks.org*
- National Parks Service – 800-365-2267, *NPS.gov*
- National Forest Service Reservation Line – 877-444-6777, *ReserveUSA.com*

Traffic / Road Conditions

- Access Atlanta Traffic Information – *AccessAtlanta.com/News/Traffic*
- Georgia DOT Road Condition Information – *404-635-6800, Georgia-Navigator.com*
- Georgia DOT Traffic Information – *404-624-1300 Ext. 1000, Georgia-Navigator.com*

Transportation

- Amtrak – 800-872-7245, *AmTrak.com*
- Atlanta Area Carpool/Vanpool Ride Share – *404-463-3100*
- Greyhound Bus – 800-231-2222, *Greyhound.com*

- Hartsfield Atlanta International Airport – *404-530-6830, Atlanta-Airport.com*
- MARTA – *404-848-4711, ItsMARTA.com*

Utility Emergencies

- Georgia Power Company (Electricity) – *888-891-0938, SouthernCo.com/GAPower*
- Atlanta Gas Light (Gas) – *770-907-4231, AtlantaGasLight.com*
- BellSouth (Phones) – *404-780-2500, BellSouth.com*
- City of Atlanta Bureau of Drinking Water – *404-658-7220, AtlantaGA.gov*
- Fulton County Water Emergency – *770-640-3040*

Venues

- The Boisfeuillet Jones Atlanta Civic Center – *404-658-7159, AtlantaCivicCenter.com*
- Chastain Amphitheatre – *404-233-7275, AtlantaConcerts.com/Chastain.html*
- Coca-Cola Lakewood Amphitheatre – *404-443-5090, LakewoodAmp.com*
- EarthLink Live – *404-885-1365, EarthlinkLive.com*
- Fox Theatre – *404-881-2100, FoxTheatre.org*
- Fox Theatre Ticket Information – *404-249-6400, FoxTheatre.org*
- The Georgia Dome – *404-233-9200, GWCC.com*
- Philips Arena – *404-249-6400, PhilipsArena.com*
- Rialto Center for the Performing Arts – *404-651-4727, RialtoCenter.org*
- Roxy Theatre – *404-233-7699*
- Woodruff Arts Center – *404-722-5000, WoodruffCenter.org*

Weather

- National Weather Service – *770-632-1837, SRH.Weather.gov*
- Weather Channel Online – *Weather.com*

Zip Codes

- *800-275-8777*
- *USPS.com*

Did You Know?

Atlanta has the tallest building in the Southeast—Bank of America Plaza—at 55 stories (1,023 feet). *600 Peachtree Street N.E., 678-553-1027, BankofAmerica.com*

about the authors

Jordan McAuley was born and raised in Atlanta. His writing has appeared in *Out, Us Weekly, Interview, HotSpots,* and *Refresh Magazine*. He is also a regular contributor to *David Magazine* and ATLANTAboy.com.

Matt Burkhalter was also born and raised in Atlanta. He has worked as a graphic designer for print publications throughout the Southeast including *The Atlanta Journal-Constitution* and *Southern Voice* newspapers.

WE'D LOVE TO HEAR FROM YOU

Please let us know your thoughts. If we left anything out or listed any incorrect information, we want to hear about it for the next edition. Contact us at *atlantaboy@gmail.com* or c/o Mega Niche Media, 925–B Peachtree Street #398, Atlanta, GA 30309. Enjoy your time in Atlanta!

index

Abbey, 53
Action Cycling Atlanta, 113
Actor's Express, 88
adult video and novelty stores, 77, 79–80
Agatha's Mystery Theatre, 88
Agave, 67–68
Agnes & Muriel's, 65–66
Aida, 88
AID Atlanta, 117
AIDS Memorial Quilt, 101, 121
AIDS Survival Project, 118
airlines, servicing Atlanta, 141
airport, 76, 150
alcohol and drug dependency services, 141
Alliance Theatre, 88
Alon's Bakery & Market, 52
Andre 3000, 26
Ansley Park, 13
Ansley Park Playhouse, 89
antique shops, 82–83
Après Diem, 53–54
area codes, 14
Armorettes, 8, 29, 31, 117
Armory, 8, 29
art museums, 99
Atlanta Ballet, 89
Atlanta Botanical Garden, 97
Atlanta Bucks Rugby Football Club, 113

Atlanta Cyclorama, 98
Atlanta Eagle, 29–30
Atlanta Exchange Network (AEN), 118
Atlanta Gay Men's Chorus, 89
Atlanta Gay Pride celebration, 17
Atlanta History Center, 97
Atlanta Opera, 90
Atlanta Pride Committee, 118
Atlanta Rainbow Trout, 113
Atlanta Symphony Orchestra, 17, 90
Atlanta Team Tennis Association, 114
Atlanta Thunder Football, 114
Atlanta Water Gardens, 75
Austin, Dallas, 26
automobile services, 142

Bacchanalia, 44, 71
Backstreet, 31
bakeries, 55
Ball, Alan, 26
ballet, 89
Baraonda, 57
barbecue, 51
bars and clubs, 29–41
Basinger, Kim, 27
"Baton Bob," 13

Bazzaar, 44–45
Bearse, Amanda, 26
bed and breakfasts, 129
bedding, 75, 77
Bed Down, 75
Belvedere, 76
Big Gay Supper Club, 73
Bikram Yoga, 105
Biltmore Hotel, 34
black bars, 30–31
Blake's On The Park, 30
blogs, 123, 124
Bodega Gardens, 82
Boisfeuillet Jones Atlanta Civic Center, 90–91
bookstores, 82
Botanical Garden, 97
Boy Next Door, 76–77
Brooks, Shawnna, 32
Brown, Bobby, 26
Brown, Charlie, 10–11
Brushstrokes, 77
Bulldogs, 30–31
Bungalow, 77
Burkhart's, 31
By Design, 77–78

cabaret, 93
Cabbagetown, 18–19
Café Intermezzo, 55
Callanwolde Art Center, 91
Candler, Asa, 19
Candler Park, 19
Cantoni, 78

capitol dome, 103
Capulets, 78
cards and stationary, 77, 81, 83
Carter, Jimmy, 100
CDC (National Center for Disease Control and Prevention), 21
celebrities, 26–27
Centennial Olympic Park, 21
Center for Puppetry Arts, 91
charitable organizations, 117–121
Charlie Brown's Cabaret, 10, 21, 31–32
Chinese restaurants, 52
CHRIS Rainbow Home, 118–119
churches, 137–139
city government, contact information, 142
civic center, 90–91
clothing stores, 76–77, 79, 85
clubs and bars, 29–41
CNN Center, 21, 98
CNN Center Studio Tour, 98
Cobalt, 109
Coca-Cola, World of, tours, 102–103
coffee shops, 52–53, 82
Cole, Kenneth, 27
Colonnade, 66
Colony Square Athletic Club, 105

Compound, 32–33
Conroy, Pat, 27
consumer complaints and services, 142–143
Convention and Visitors Bureau, 149
Cook's Warehouse, 78
Cotton States International Exhibition, 15, 16
county government, contact information, 143
Cowtippers, 72
Cuban restaurants, 54–55
cycling, 113
Cyclorama, 98

Dad's Garage, 91–92
dance clubs, 29, 30, 32, 33, 34, 35–36, 37
Daniels, Heather, 32
Decalur, 20
Decatur, Stephen, 20
DeGarmo, Diana, 26
delicatessens, 52
Designing Women, 35
desserts, restaurants featuring, 55
discrimination, government agencies concerned with, 143–144
Doc Chey's, 63
Dogwood Festival, 17
Dorff, Stephen, 27
downtown, 20–21

drag shows, 30, 31–32, 38, 59–60
Driving Miss Daisy, 22
Druid Hills, 22
Dupri, Jermaine, 26, 27
Dusty's Barbecue, 51

Ebenezer Baptist Church, 101
Eclipse di Luna, 69
ED's gourmet records, 78–79
eighties music, 38
Einstein's, 45
El Chaparral, 33
eleven50, 33
Emory University, 27
Eno, 60
entertainment resources, 144–145, 150
Eric Low Salon, 109
ethnic mix of Atlanta population, 14
events
 listing by month, 131–135
 at Piedmont Park, 16–18

Fanning, Dakota, 26
Fat Matt's Rib Shack, 51
Fellini's Pizza, 64
Fernbank Museum of Natural History, 98
Fernbank Science Center & Observatory, 99
Ferst Center for the Arts, 92
Figo Pasta, 57–58

Fishmonger, 64–65
fitness centers, 105–107
Fitness Factory, 105–106
flag-football team, 114
Floataway Café, 58
florists, 81, 84–85
Flying Biscuit, 66–67
Fonda, Jane, 18, 26
football, 114
14th Street Playhouse, 87
Fox Theatre, 92, 99
Foxworthy, Jeff, 27
French Kiss, 79
Fresche Hair Studio, 109
Fried Green Tomatoes, 65
Frog's Cantina, 68
Frontrunners, 114
Fulton Bag & Cotton Mill, 18–19
furniture and home accessories stores, 76, 77–78, 80, 81, 82, 83, 84, 85
Future, 34

garbage and sanitation services, 144
gardening stores and nurseries, 75, 79
Gay Activist Alliance, 17
Gay Liberation Front, 17
Gay Men's Chorus, 89
Gay Pride, 16–17, 118
Georgia Equality, 119
Georgia State University, 21

Georgia Tech, 92, 106
gift stores, 77, 81, 83, 84–85
Gilbert's Mediterranean Café, 60–61
Gone with the Wind, 48, 100
Grace, Nancy, 27
Grant, Lemuel P., 22
Grant Central Pizza, 64
Grant Park, 22–23
The Grape, 61
grocery stores, 70–71
gyms, 105–107

Habersham Gardens, 79
Halo, 34
hamburger joints, 56
Harold, Gale, 27
Harrison, Randy, 27
Hartsfield-Jackson International Airport, 76, 150
health care, telephone numbers, 145
health clubs, 105–107
Helmet, 110
Heretic, 35
Highlands, 25
High Museum of Art, 99
hip hop, 30
History Center of Atlanta, 97
Hoedowns, 35–36
Hogan, Hulk, 27
Horizon Theatre, 92–93
hostels, 129
hotels, 127–129

Hotlanta Soccer Association, 114
Hotlanta Softball, 115
Hotlanta Volleyball Association, 115
Houston, Whitney, 26
Howell, John, 25
Hulk Hogan, 27
Hunter, Holly, 27
Hurt, Joel, 23–24

ice cream, 56
IMAX Theater, 98
Indigo Girls, 20, 26
Inman Park, 23–24
Inserection, 79–80
Intaglia, 80
Interior Dimensions, 80
Italian restaurants, 57–59

Jackson, Janet, 26
Jake's Ice Cream, 56
James Madison Salon, 110
Jimmy Carter Library & Museum, 24, 100
Joe's East Atlanta Coffee Shop, 53
Joe's On Juniper, 49
John, Elton, 26, 88
John Howell Park, 25
Joiner, Rusty, 27
JOQ Day Spa, 110
Jungle Club, 36
Junkman's Daughter, 80

karaoke, 37
Kenneth Cole, 27
Kenny's Alley, 36
Key Lime Pie, 110
King, Coretta Scott, 100
King, Martin Luther, Jr., 100–101, 103
King Center, 100
King Plow Arts Center, 88
Kruiz, Ashley, 32

L.A. Fitness, 106
Lake Clara Meer, 15
Las Palmeras, 54–55
Latin music, 33, 38
Lee, Spike, 27
legal referral services, 146
LeMasters, Lauren, 32
Lenox Square, 81
Libby's Cabaret, 93
libraries, 146
Licious, Bubba D., 8–9
Ligne Roset, 81
line-dancing, 35–36
linens, 75, 77
Little Azio, 58–59
Little Bangkok, 52
Little Five Points, 24–25
Little Richard, 27
Lively, Eric, 26
Loca Luna, 69–70
The Loft, 37
Ludacris, 26
Lust, Lena, 32

magazine resources, 123–125
mail service, 147
Majestic Diner, 43–44
malls, shopping, 81, 83
maps
    metro, 4–5
    midtown, 6–7
Margaret Mitchell House & Museum, 100
The Mark Ultralounge, 37
MARTA (Metropolitan Atlanta Rapid Transit Authority), 16, 101, 150
Mary Mac's Tea Room, 67
Mary's, 37–38
The Masquerade, 38
Mayer, John, 27
medical care, telephone numbers, 145
Mediterranean restaurants, 60–61
Metro, 38
Metropolitan Deluxe, 81
Metrotainment Bakery, 55
Mexican/Southwestern restaurants, 61–63, 67–69
midtown
    Ansley Park neighborhood, 13
    map of, 6–7
Midtown Art Cinema, 93
Miss Q's, 38–39
Mitchell, Margaret, 19, 48, 100
Moe's Southwest Grill, 68

Morehouse College, 27
motels and hotels, 127–129
movie theaters, 18, 93
Mullins, Shawn, 26, 27
Murphy's, 49–50
music stores, 77, 78–79, 84

Naked Boys Singing, 29
Nam, 73
Names Project Foundation, Inc., 101, 121
National Center for Disease Control and Prevention (CDC), 21
Natural History Museum, 98
Neighborhood Playhouse, 93–94
networking organizations, 118
New American Shakespeare Tavern, 94
New Order, 39
newspaper resources, 123–125
Nickiemoto's, 59
No Mas Productions, 82
Noodle, 63
noodle houses, 63
Nuevo Laredo Cantina, 61–62
nurseries and gardening stores, 75, 79

Oakland Cemetery, 65
observatory, 98

Olmsted, Frederick Law, 15, 22
Olmsted Brothers, 23
O'Neal, Shaquille, 26
ONE.Midtown Kitchen, 45–46
opera, 90
orchestra, 17, 90
The Oscar's, 39
Osteria 832, 59
Outkast, 25, 26
Outwrite Bookstore and Coffeehouse, 82

P.A.L.S., 119
Paris on Ponce, 82–83
parking violations, 146
parks
    John Howell Park, 25
    Piedmont Park, 13, 14–18
    resources, 146
    Springvale Park, 23
Peachtree, streets named, 27
Peachtree Playhouse, 94
pets, 141
Pets are Loving Support (P.A.L.S.), 119
PFLAG Atlanta, 120
Phipps Plaza, 83
phoenix, as city symbol, 21, 132
The Phoenix (bar), 40
Piedmont Driving Club, 14
Piedmont Park, 13, 14–18
pizza, 57, 64
planetarium, 98
Pleasant Peasant, 46
police departments, 143, 146–147
population, 14
Poster Hut, 83
post office, 147
Pride celebration, 16–17, 118
Project Open Hand, 120
Puck, Wolfgang, 48–49
puppetry, 91
Pushpush Theater, 94–95

Queer as Folk, 27
quilt, memorial AIDS, 101, 121

Rainbow Home, 118–119
Rainbow Trout aquatics club, 113
Rathburn's Restaurant, 46
Raven, 32
Raven Symone, 27
Ray, Amy, 26
The Real World, 63
recycling, 147
Red Chair Restaurant, 70
Red Chair Video Lounge, 40
religious services, 137–139
restaurants
    American-contemporary, 44–49
    American-traditional, 49–51
    barbecue, 51

bistro/deli, 52
Chinese, 52
coffee shops, 52–53, 82
continental, 53–54
Cuban, 54–55
dessert, 55–56
hamburgers, 56
Italian, 57–59
Mediterranean, 60–61
Mexican, 61–63
noodle houses, 63
pizza, 57, 64
seafood, 64–65
Southern food, 65–67
Southwestern, 67–69
steakhouses, 72
sushi, 59–60
tapas, 69–70
Thai, 72
24-hour diners, 43–44
Vietnamese, 73
Retromodern, 83
Richie Arpino Salon, 110–111
road conditions, 149
Roberts, Danny, 63
Roberts, Julia, 27
rugby, 113
running clubs, 114
RuPaul, 27
Ru San's, 60

salons and spas, 109–111
Schneider, Fred, 26
Science Center & Observatory, 99
Scream Boutique, 83
Screen on the Green, 18
Seacrest, Ryan, 27
seafood restaurants, 64–65
Sevananda, 70
7 Stages, 87
Shakespeare Tavern, 94
Sherman, General William, 20
shipping services, 147
Shoemaker's Warehouse, 83–84
shopping, 75–85
show tunes, 39
Silk, 52
Six Feet Under, 65
Six Feet Under, 26
Six Flags Over Georgia, 101
Six Flags White Water, 101–102
Skate Escape, 84
soccer, 114
softball, 115
Solarium, 111
Southern food, 65–67
Southwestern/Mexican restaurants, 61–63, 67–69
Space, 84
spas, 109, 110
Spice, 47
sports bars, 41
sports clubs, 113–115

sports teams and events, contact information, 147–148
Springvale Park, 23
Star Provisions, 70–71
state government, contact information, 148
stationary and cards, 77, 81, 83
steakhouses, 72
Stone Mountain Park, 102
strip clubs, 40–41
Sun Dial Restaurant, Bar & View, 47
sushi, 59–60
swimming clubs, 113
Swinging Richards, 40–41
Symone, Raven, 27

tanning salons, 111
tapas restaurants, 69–70
Taqueria del Sol, 68–69
taxi service, 148–149
TBS (Turner Broadcasting System), 21
tea rooms, 67
temperature, averages, 14
tennis, 114
Thai Chili, 72
Thai restaurants, 52, 72
theater, 87–89, 91–95
Thomas, Rozonda "Chilli," 27
Thumbs Up, 50
"Thump," 33

time zone, 14
TLC, 26, 27
Toast, 47
tourist information, 149
traffic conditions, 149
transportation, 149–150
travel services, 149
Turner, Ted, 26
Turner Broadcasting System (TBS), 21
Twelve, 84–85
24-hour diners, 43–44
Two.Urban Licks, 48

Uncle Julio's Casa Grande, 62
Underground Atlanta, 21–22, 36
Universal Gear, 85
Urban Body Fitness, 106–107
Usher, 26, 27
utilities, 150

Van Michael, 111
Varsity Restaurant, 57
Vickery's Bar & Grill, 48
video bars, 35, 39, 40
Vietnamese restaurants, 73
Virginia-Highlands, 25
volleyball, 115
Vortex Bar & Grill, 56

Waffle House, 44
walking tours, 102
Water Gardens, Atlanta, 75

water parks, 101–102
weather, 14, 151
Web sites, 123–125
West Egg Café, 50–51
WETbar, 41
Whole Foods Market, 71
Whole World Theatre, 95
Willy's Mexicana Grill, 62
wine bars, 60, 61
Winfrey, Oprah, 15
Wolfgang Puck Express, 48–49
Woodruff Arts Center, 88
Woof's on Piedmont, 41

Yes, 85
yoga, 105, 106
Youth Pride, 120

zip code information, 151
Zocalo, 62–63
Zoo Atlanta, 103

order form

Please send me _____ copies of *ATLANTAboy* at $9.95 each plus $5.00 shipping ($7.00 international).

Name: _____

Address: _____

City: _____ State: _____ Zip _____

Country: _____

Phone: _____

Email: _____

TOTAL ENCLOSED: $ _____

PAYMENT METHOD: ☐ Check/Money Order

For credit card orders please call 1-800-BOOKLOG or order online at ATLANTAboy.com.

Mail to: Mega Niche Media
925-B Peachtree Street #398
Atlanta, GA 30309

Phone: 1-800-BOOKLOG (24 hours)
Online: ATLANTAboy.com or Amazon.com
or special order at your local bookstore.

notes

notes

notes